ROUTLEDGE LIBRARY EDITIONS: ACCOUNTING HISTORY

Volume 20

THE EVOLUTION OF CONSOLIDATED FINANCIAL REPORTING IN AUSTRALIA

THE EVOLUTION OF CONSOLIDATED FINANCIAL REPORTING IN AUSTRALIA

An Evaluation of Alternative Hypotheses

GREG WHITTRED

LONDON AND NEW YORK

First published in 1988 by Garland Publishing, Inc.

This edition first published in 2021
by Routledge
2 Park Square, Milton Park, Abingdon, Oxon OX14 4RN

and by Routledge
52 Vanderbilt Avenue, New York, NY 10017

Routledge is an imprint of the Taylor & Francis Group, an informa business

British Library Cataloguing in Publication Data
A catalogue record for this book is available from the British Library

ISBN: 978-0-367-33564-9 (Set)
ISBN: 978-1-00-304636-3 (Set) (ebk)
ISBN: 978-0-367-49696-8 (Volume 20) (hbk)
ISBN: 978-0-367-49697-5 (Volume 20) (pbk)
ISBN: 978-1-00-304700-1 (Volume 20) (ebk)

Publisher's Note
The publisher has gone to great lengths to ensure the quality of this reprint but points out that some imperfections in the original copies may be apparent.

Disclaimer
The publisher has made every effort to trace copyright holders and would welcome correspondence from those they have been unable to trace.

The Evolution of Consolidated Financial Reporting in Australia

An Evaluation of Alternative Hypotheses

GREG WHITTRED

GARLAND PUBLISHING, INC.

NEW YORK & LONDON 1988

For a list of Garland's publications in accounting, see the final pages of this volume.

Library of Congress Cataloging in Publication Data

Whittred, Greg.
The evolution of consolidated financial reporting in Austrailia : an evaluation of alternative hypotheses / Greg Whittred.
p. cm. — (Foundations of accounting)
Bibliography: p.
ISBN 0-8240-6122-5 (alk. paper)
1. Financial statements. Consolidated—Australia. 2. Holding companies—Australia—Accounting. 3. Corporations—Taxation—Australia—Consolidated returns. I. Title. II. Series.
HF5681.B2W468 1988
657'.3'0994—dc 19 88-17508

Design by Renata Gomes

The volumes in this series are printed on acid-free, 250-year-life paper.

Printed in the United States of America

INDEX

Chapter Page

ACKNOWLEDGEMENTS

This manuscript is based on my Ph.D. thesis at the Australian Graduate School of Management, University of New South Wales. I would like to acknowledge the guidance and assistance of my thesis supervisors, Ray Ball and Peter Dodd. Earlier drafts of this manuscript benefited from the detailed comments of Ross Watts, Philip Brown, Ian Zimmer and David Emanuel.

LIST OF ILLUSTRATIONS

LIST OF TABLES

CHAPTER 1

INTRODUCTION

In their attempt to develop a theory of the ownership structure of firms Jensen and Meckling (1976) define the concept of agency costs, investigate the nature of the agency costs generated by the existence of debt and outside equity and demonstrate who bears these costs and why. In the process the central role of monitoring and bonding activities in reducing agency costs becomes apparent. In this respect, Jensen and Meckling (p.338) provide an example of the way in which audited financial statements might reduce agency costs:

> Suppose, for example, that the bond holders (or outside equity holders) would find it worthwhile to produce detailed financial statements such as those contained in the usual published accounting reports as a means of monitoring the manager. If the manager himself can produce such information at lower costs than they (perhaps because he is already collecting much of the data they desire for his own internal decision making purposes), it would pay him to agree in advance to incur the cost of providing such reports and to have their accuracy testified to by an independent outside auditor.

Watts (1977) pursues the theme that the function of audited financial statements is to reduce agency costs and provides a number of hypotheses which illustrate the manner in which the agency framework might be employed to explain both the existence of financial statements and cross-sectional variation in the content thereof.

Jensen and Meckling imply and Watts hypothesises that audited financial statements are likely to be part of any contracting equilibrium in which agency costs are potentially high. However, neither Jensen and Meckling nor Watts confront their hypothesis with evidence on other than a casual basis. While doing so was beyond the scope of their analyses the result has been a lack of evidence on what is an important maintained hypothesis in much of the subsequent "positive" research in accounting - particularly that relating to accounting method choice.[1]

This study to provides evidence on the voluntary adoption of a particular type of financial statement - the consolidated financial statement - in what may be characterized as relatively high agency cost situations. Further, and in contrast to prior studies which, with one exception,[2] investigate management's policy choices taking existing contracts (and the accounting choices available under them) as given; this study examines an accounting method choice not under the assumption that it will be made opportunistically but under the assumption that it will be negotiated ex ante as part of the firm's optimal contract structure.

1.1 ORGANISATION OF THE STUDY

Chapter 2 reviews the development of consolidated financial reporting in Australia, and in particular, New South Wales (N.S.W.) and Victoria. Since financial reporting in Australia has

---

1. This is not to suggest that empirical evidence is entirely lacking. Recent papers by Leftwich, Watts and Zimmerman (1981) and Chow (1982) consider the derived demand for interim reports and auditors respectively (both monitoring devices), as a function of agency costs. The latter provides evidence consistent with this view. Leftwich (1983) and Whittred and Zimmer (1985) provide evidence regarding the degree of dependence of, respectively, private and public debt contracts on the information contained in financial statements.

2. Refer Zimmer (1986) and Chapter 4 infra.

been governed by rules developed from a variety of sources for quite some time considerable effort is expended in identifying a sample(s) of companies that may be described as consolidating in the absence of any specific institutional requirements to do so. As a by-product of this effort empirical evidence on (a) the reporting practices of Australian companies over the period 1930-1962 and (b) the extent of compliance with various institutional reporting requirements is, for the first time, made available.

Chapter 3 traces briefly the evolution of Australian capital markets and, in particular, the market for debt. The discussion here demonstrates that the rapid spread of the consolidated form of financial reporting coincided with the freeing up of the market for equity capital and the development of a market for public debt. This chapter also provides the rationale for a three way partitioning of the 1930-1962 time period which is employed in the empirical analysis.

Chapter 4 examines the determinants of management's decision to consolidate. The nature of the contracting problems confronting management and the suppliers of both debt and equity capital are considered. In both cases the solutions likely to be negotiated (ex ante) to these contracting problems imply consolidated financial reporting will be part of the equilibrium outcome. The alternative hypothesis that consolidation is a manisfestation of ex post opportunistic behaviour by management is also considered.

Chapter 5 discusses the research design and related considerations, including data collection procedures. A conventional non-equivalent control group design is employed to analyse the data. A case study approach is also used to supplement the analysis. Chapter 6 provides a profile analysis of the resulting samples and the results of the hypothesis tests. The analysis is conducted over varying time periods. The data is initially partitioned into pre- and post- disclosure regulation samples (though all the latter companies were technically exempt from the requirement to consolidate). Based on a 1941 cut-off this provides samples of 10 and 70 companies respectively. The post-disclosure regulation sample is subsequently partitioned into two periods 1941-1951 and 1952-1962. This split is based on the fact that institutional changes in 1950-51 (the effective removal of Capital Issues Controls and changes in the tax system) imply non-stationarities in some of the independent variables.

Chapter 7 is devoted to a consideration of a number of alternative hypotheses for the phenomenon under consideration. Hypotheses are developed pertaining to the possibility that the practices of particular auditing firms or overseas influences may be responsible for management's decision to consolidate. Taxation related incentives to consolidate may also exist and much of this chapter is devoted to a detailed consideration of this issue. As a result of this analysis evidence is presented (again for the first time) on the evolution of the holding company form in Australia and the importance of tax considerations therein.

Chapter 8 contains a summary and the principal conclusions reached. The research reported herein suggests that consolidation was more likely to be adopted in high agency cost situations i.e., those in which cross-guarantees between related corporations were present and/or in which management's share of a firm's equity was relatively small. The likelihood of consolidation was also a function of the number and type of subsidiaries. With the exception of the separation of ownership from control of the firm the relative significance of these factors was time dependent. The agency or contracting cost variables overwhelmed all others in terms of explanatory power, though it is apparent they were not the sole determinant of the consolidation decision.

CHAPTER 2

THE DEVELOPMENT OF CONSOLIDATED FINANCIAL REPORTING IN AUSTRALIA

Corporate financial reporting in Australia has, for at least the last 60 years, been subject to rules developed from various sources. In this respect the provisions of the various Companies Acts, the listing requirements of the Australian Associated Stock Exchanges and, more recently, the standards issued by the professional accounting bodies (the Australian Society of Accountants and the Institute of Chartered Accountants in Australia) have all assumed importance. For much of this time holding companies' financial statements have been accompanied by consolidated financial statements. Yet, it is possible to identify time periods in Australian history when these institutional requirements did not exist and in which companies were consolidating.[1] The identification of such time periods and companies is the purpose of this chapter. However, before proceeding to this task the scope of the search is restricted by confining attention to the States of N.S.W. and Victoria. These States have always been the most heavily populated and their capitals, Sydney and Melbourne, became at a very early stage the financial and commercial centres of Australia. For this reason (and for more practical considerations pertaining to data availability) attention hereafter is focussed upon developments in each of these States.

---

1. It could also be argued (following Posner (1977)) that the institutional framework evolved in order to facilitate private contracting arrangements. Tests of this hypothesis are beyond the scope of this study.

The chapter is structured as follows. The evolution of the rules from each of the institutional sources referred to above is reviewed in section 2.1. This allows the identification of a set of sample parameters or selection criteria which are discussed in section 2.2. Finally, section 2.3 documents the evolution of the consolidation practices of Australian companies. This survey provides the initial data base from which sample members are ultimately drawn.

2.1 INSTITUTIONAL REQUIREMENTS

2.1.1 Legislative Provisions

The practice of consolidated financial reporting in Australia lagged by some 10-20 years corresponding developments in the United Kingdom (U.K.) and by some 30-40 years American practice.[2] The first set of consolidated accounts issued by an Australian public company appeared no later than 1931.[3] However, the legislative provisions of certain States and in particular the 1938 Victorian Companies Act anticipated British legislation in

---

2. Nobel Industries (1922) is generally credited with being the first U.K. consolidation (e.g., Nobes and Parker, 1979, p.199; Kitchen, 1972, p.126/7). However, Edwards and Webb (1984, p.38) provide evidence of U.K. companies consolidating as early as 1910. Nevertheless, it remained the case that the publication of consolidated financial statements was the exception rather than the rule throughout the 1920's. (Edwards and Webb, 1984, p.32; Walker, 1978, Chapter 6). Mumford (1982) provides evidence of U.S. companies consolidating as early as 1890. The development of consolidated reporting in the U.K. is reviewed in Kitchen (1972) and Walker (1978); in the U.S.A. by Walker (1978) and Mumford (1982); and in Australia by Gibson (1971). The latter author also documents in considerable detail the evolution of the legislative and Stock Exchange reporting requirements in Australia.

3. This is some four years earlier than the date documented by Gibson (1971) - refer section 2.3 infra and footnote 14.

this area by a decade. A Companies Bill had been introduced into the Victorian parliament in 1935 and after a three year passage passed into law on December 7, 1938.[4] While still requiring a balance sheet the Victorian Act departed from the practice of its predecessors of specifying a format in the schedules. For the first time (in either the U.K. or Australia) a detailed profit and loss statement was required (Sn. 125(1)(a)). Finally the Act required, again for the first time, either separate statements (in the prescribed detail) for each subsidiary or the inclusion with the parent company accounts of the consolidated statements of the parent and its subsidiaries (Sn. 125 (1) (b)).[5]

The 1938 Act was followed by Western Australia in 1943 and was revised in 1958; this revision being adopted in Tasmania in 1959. However, similar requirements did not appear in the legislative provisions of the remaining Australian States until the Uniform Companies Act, 1961. In fact the requirements in the remaining states were modelled on those of the U.K. Companies Act, 1929 which was the first Act to require the disclosure of certain aspects of holding company affairs. Companies covered by this act were obliged to separately disclose investments in subsidiaries,

---

4. Gibson (1971, Chapter 5) describes the passage of this Bill and its "radical" requirements as tumultuous.

5. The definition of subsidiary company contained in the Act was sufficiently broad to cover sub-subsidiaries. However, it did not require that the accounts of the subsidiaries be made up to the same date as those of the holding company or the separate disclosure of minority interests. Further, the Act permitted the exclusion of subsidiaries incorporated outside Victoria so long as their separate balance sheets were appended. The latter had only to comply with the disclosure requirements prevailing in their State of incorporation (Ewart, 1948).

the amounts due to and from subsidiaries, and to provide a statement of how the profits of the subsidiaries were dealt with but not the amount of these profits. Identical provisions were written into the New South Wales Companies Act, 1936 (Sns. 105, 106) and as observed above, remained in force until the Uniform Companies Act, 1961.

As in the Victorian Companies Act, 1938 the Uniform Companies Act, 1961 (Ninth Schedule, 4(1)) required of every holding company either separate financial statements for each subsidiary or the consolidation of the company and its subsidiaries i.e., consolidated accounts. The 1961 Act was amended in 1971. The revisions followed the British example and required group accounts defined as (Sn. 161):

(i) one set of consolidated accounts of a group;
(ii) two or more sets of consolidated accounts covering a group;
(iii) separate accounts for each corporation in a group; and
(iv) a combination of one or more sets of consolidated accounts and one or more separate accounts together covering a group.

These provisions remain unchanged in the respective Companies Codes, 1981. As in the U.K. (refer footnote 2) the presentation of anything other than (i) was (and remains) relatively uncommon.

2.1.2 Stock Exchange Provisions

The preceding discussion traces the development of the legislative requirements regarding holding company disclosure. Yet in Australia the first attempt to deal with this issue came from the Stock Exchanges. The Sydney and Melbourne Stock Exchanges first issued codified Listing Requirements in November 1925. Clause D(32) and D(28) (Sydney and Melbourne respectively) thereof required:

> That any company that has a controlling interest in another Company or Companies, shall with its own balance-sheet furnish shareholders with balance-sheets and profit and loss accounts of the subsidiary Company or Companies.

In December 1927 the Melbourne Exchange amended this requirement to give companies the option of submitting either separate subsidiary accounts or an aggregate balance sheet and profit and loss account of the subsidiaries.[6] The Sydney Exchange also amended its requirements in July 1927 and, at least temporarily, the requirements of the two Exchanges departed. The Sydney amendments required that a holding company may submit an aggregate balance sheet and profit and loss account of the company and the subsidiaries in lieu of the separate financial statements.[7] In 1936 these requirements were realigned with those in Melbourne.[8] Subsequent to the Victorian Companies Act 1938, both Exchanges adopted (June 1941) a requirement that holding companies attach to their financial statements either separate statements for each subsidiary or consolidated statements for the group.[9] In Victoria

---

6. Official List Requirements (Melbourne) - December 1927, D(34). These statements were simply an "aggregation" of the individual subsidiaries accounts and two points are worth noting. First, they excluded the parent company's accounts. Second, none of the usual inter-company eliminations and adjustments that identify a "consolidation" were performed (Nixon, 1928, p.364; Fitzgerald, 1938, p.142 and Fitzgerald, 1939, p.87).

7. Official List Requirements (Sydney) - July 1927, D(34). Once again the statements were an "aggregation" and not a "consolidation" (refer footnote 6).

8. Official List Requirements (Sydney) - July 1936, D(43).

9. Official List Requirements (Sydney, Melbourne) - June 1941, D(43).

this represented an aligning of Stock Exchange requirements with those of the relevant companies legislation. For N.S.W. holding companies it represented a new reporting requirement. However, as with all amendments to the Listing Requirements until 1954, its effect was restricted to holding companies subsequently seeking listing. It was not until September 1946 that companies applying for listing in either Sydney or Melbourne were required to enter into a "form of agreement" to abide by the Stock Exchanges' Official List Requirements. In 1954 this "form of agreement" was amended to include a "dragnet" clause aimed at making future amendments to the list requirements retrospective.

2.1.3 Accounting Standards

There have been few professional pronouncements on the matter of consolidated statements in Australia. The first such statement appeared in May, 1946 when the General Council of the Institute of Chartered Accountants approved the publication of five "Recommendations on Accounting Principles". Included fifth among these was one entitled "Disclosure of the Financial Position and Results of Subsidiary Companies in the Accounts of Holding Companies"; which was identical to that of the 1944 English Institute's pronouncement of the same title. It was not until 1956 that any statement on consolidation appeared under the auspices of the Australian Society of Accountants. This statement was entitled "Notes on the Preparation of Consolidated Statements" and was distributed as a supplement to the April issue of The Australian Accountant. Revised and reissued in 1968 as Society Bulletin No.2, it retained the same format as its predecessor though it covered a greater number of points. The statement remained, however, strictly the views of the specially appointed (N.S.W.) research committee.

Both the Institute's and the Society's efforts retain the status of Recommendations on Accounting Practice. There are no accounting standards on this area in Australia. However, consolidation is presently on the agenda of the standard setting authorities and the regulatory agencies concerned with corporate reporting.[10]

2.2 IDENTIFICATION OF VOLUNTARY CONSOLIDATORS

Based on the preceding discussion Figure 2.1 summarizes the "reporting requirements" in force at various points in time in both N.S.W. and Victoria. It is apparent that the "requirement" to consolidate first appeared as an option in the Victorian Companies Act, 1938. A consolidation requirement did not appear in N.S.W. until the 1941 revision of the Sydney Stock Exchange Listing requirements - and again it appeared as an option. The contemporaneous revision of the Melbourne list requirements meant that both Stock Exchanges' requirements had been brought into line with those of the Victorian Act. Note however that (in contrast to the Victorian situation) a consolidation requirement did not appear in the NSW legislation until July, 1962 when the N.S.W.

---

10. The Australian Accounting Research Foundation (AARF) has recently released Discussion Paper No.8, Accounting for Business Combinations and another on "Consolidations" is being prepared (McGregor, 1984, p.867). The Accounting Standards Review Board received a submission from the Australian Shareholder's Association on the "area of consolidation" in August, 1984. In December 1984 the Board indicated (ASRB Release 300 pp.6-7) its intention to refer the submission to the AARF for comment before commencing its review.

FIGURE 1

Time Series of Reporting Obligations

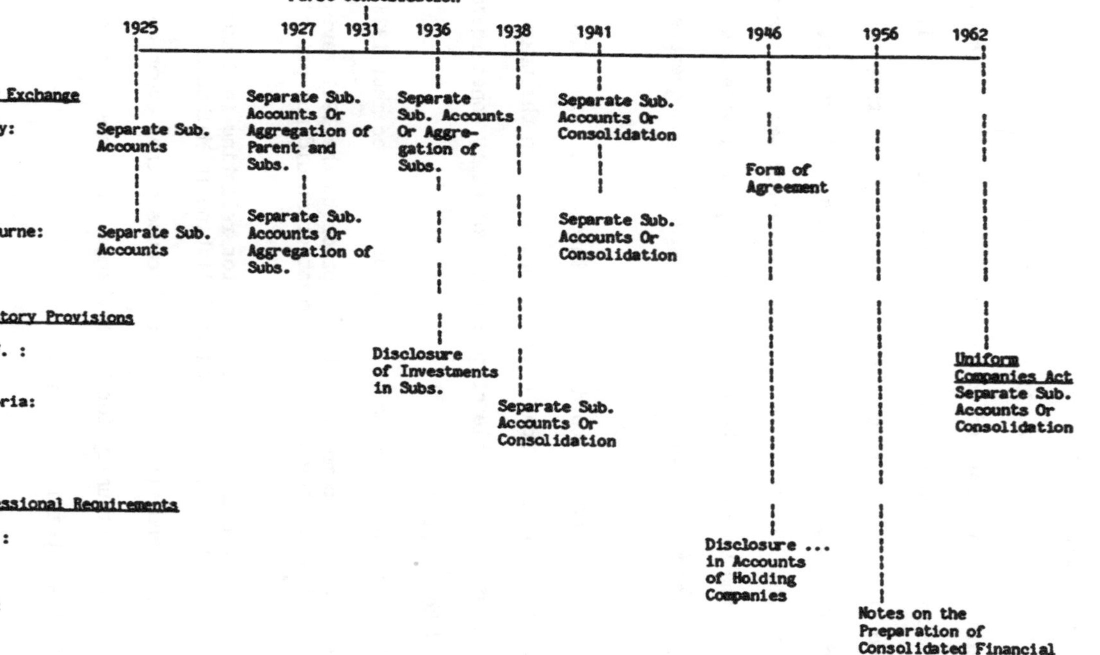

Companies Act, 1961 became effective.

Indeed, prior to 1962 it is not clear what obligation N.S.W. companies felt themselves under to change their reporting practices. First, the listing requirements only applied to companies being admitted to the list after 1941. Second, even then it was not until 1946 that companies entering the list were obliged to sign a "form of agreement" in which they explicitly agreed to comply with these requirements. Third, it is not obvious what the penalties for non compliance were or (as in the case of the Victorian Act) how vigorously compliance was policed or, perhaps more importantly, what were the consequences of non-compliance.

It is possible to draw some inferences regarding these matters from the empirical evidence presented in the next section. At this stage the sample of potential voluntary consolidators is defined to include:

(a) Victorian companies listed prior to December 1938; and

(b) N.S.W. companies listed prior to the 1941 revision of the Sydney list requirements that did not prior to 1962 either:

 (i) reorganize and apply for relisting in Sydney, or
 (ii) apply for concurrent listing in Melbourne.

Criteria b(i) and (ii) are imposed because either event could have provided an opportunity for the Exchanges to compel a change in an applicant's reporting behaviour.

2.3 THE HISTORICAL EXPERIENCE

This section presents empirical evidence regarding the evolution of consolidated financial reporting in Australia. In this context it is apparent from section 2.1 that the decade of the 1930s is an important one. Consequently the period 1930-40 inclusive is analysed in some detail. However, the financial reporting practices of "holding companies" are also considered at a number of other points in time. The selection of these points was dictated by the nature of available historical data sources.

The principal source of the data in this section is <u>Jobson's Investment Digest</u>. The <u>Digest</u> was first published in January, 1920. From its first volume up until February, 1954 the <u>Digest</u> adopted the policy of reproducing (in their entirety) company balance sheets issued during the preceding month. It defined its population in its first editorial as shares listed on Commonwealth of Australia Stock Exchanges.

The <u>Digest</u> thus provides an accessible source of company balance sheets for most of the period of concern in this thesis (i.e., 1930-1962). In order to collect empirical evidence on the development of consolidated financial reporting in Australia every issue of the <u>Digest</u> for the calendar years 1920, 1930-40 and 1953 was surveyed with a view to identifying the relative frequency of consolidation in both N.S.W. and Victoria - both before and after the introduction of the major institutional reporting requirements discussed above. For reasons which will become apparent in Chapter 4.4.3 data was also collected for the remaining years indicated in Table 2.1.

Table 2.1 provides a frequency distribution (proportions in parentheses) by year and State of the number of consolidators identifiable from the Digest.[11] The denominator in these calculations is intended to be the number of holding companies (i.e., possible consolidators) in each State. The Table also includes frequency distributions for the two other types of disclosure adopted by holding companies (separate subsidiary accounts or an aggregate statement of the assets and liabilities of subsidiaries). Appendix I contains complete reporting histories of listed Companies that adopted some form of extended disclosure regarding their subsidiaries over the period 1930-1940 inclusive.

Before discussing the survey results one important caveat is required. Prior to 1936 in N.S.W. (1938 in Victoria) there was no legal requirement for holding companies to separately disclose the existence of any investment in subsidiaries in their accounts (refer 2.1.1 above). The denominator in the calculation of the percentage of consolidators in each State prior to these points in time must therefore be regarded with some caution. Only those companies that could unambiguously be identified as having subsidiaries - either because of an explicit disclosure in the accounts or from the discussion in the accompanying investment review - were included. This procedure likely understates the number of holding companies, thereby overstating the proportion of

11. Only N.S.W. and Victoria are included in Table 2.1 because with the exception of two companies (identified in Appendix I) there were no consolidators in the remaining Australian states over the 1920-40 period. However, by 1953 approximately 43 percent of the holding companies from these States were consolidating.

TABLE 2.1

Financial Reporting Practice of N.S.W. and Victorian Companies
Financial Year Ending in Calender 1930-1953
Number (%)

Year	State/Type of Disclosure					
	New South Wales			Victoria		
	Separate Sub. Accounts	Aggregate Accounts of Subsidiaries	Consolidation (%)	Separate Sub. Accounts	Aggregate Accounts of Subsidiaries	Consolidation (%)
1920	2	0	0(0.0)	0	0	0(0.0)
1930	0	1	0(0.0)	4	2	0(0.0)
1931	0	2	0(0.0)	4	3	1(4.2)
1932	0	1	0(0.0)	4	2	2(8.7)
1933	1	1	0(0.0)	5	2	2(8.0)
1934	2	2	0(0.0)	5	2	2(6.9)
1935	2	2	1(3.3)	4	2	3(7.9)
1936	2	2	1(3.3)	4	2	3(9.9)
1937	1	3	3(3.7)	2	3	4(13.8)
1938	3	5	2(2.4)	5	4	6(13.6)
1939	3	5	3(3.3)	2	0	25(39.1)
1940	5	5	3(4.1)	3	0	39(50.6)
1941	0	0	5(6.9)	1	0	18(31.0)
1943	0	0	6(6.3)	1	0	26(35.1)
1947	0	2	18(23.7)	0	0	57(74.0)
1950	0	0	32(32.0)	0	0	74(78.7)
1953	0	0	74(60.2)	0	0	70(81.4)

consolidators in any given year.[12]

Table 2.1 indicates the first consolidation in Australia occurred in 1931 - some 4 years prior to the date indicated in Gibson (1971, p.312)[13] or Ma and Parker (1983, p.7). Appendix I identifies the first company to consolidate in Australia as Hoyts Theatres Ltd. (Vic., 1931). Further, at least 2 other companies (Lincoln Mills (Australia) Ltd., Vic., 1932 and Adelaide Motors Ltd, South Australia, 1934) consolidated prior to Dunlop.

It is apparent from Table 2.1 that prior to the introduction of the first consolidation requirement in N.S.W. in 1941 only 4 percent of holding companies had adopted this practice. Across all three forms of extended disclosure this figure rises to approximately 17 per cent. Only 4 separate N.S.W. companies consolidated at any time over the period 1931-1940. It is also apparent that subsequent to the introduction of this listing requirement and prior to the incorporation of a similar requirement in the legislation in 1962 there was a gradual increase in the proportion of holding companies consolidating in

---

12. It is difficult to gauge the extent of this bias. In any year up to twice as many companies disclosed they had "shares/investments in other companies" as disclosed they had "shares/investments in subsidiaries." Note that in the present context the bias will only be important if it is manifested in a differential propensity to disclose "shares/investments in subsidiaries" in the two States.

13. Gibson (1971 p.312) indicates that Dunlop Perdriau Rubber Co. Ltd, in 1935, was the first Australian company to consolidate. However, at p.140 he states the year was 1937. Correspondence with this author (dated 16 July, 1984) reveals the latter date to be a misprint. It is also worth noting that the first Australian consolidation (1931) occurred some twenty years after that in the U.K. (refer footnote 2), though two years prior to the much celebrated 1933 Dunlop Ltd accounts in England (Kitchen and Parker, 1980, pp.98-109).

N.S.W. This observation appears to be consistent with the views of Ewart (1948, p.487), Fitzgerald (1944, p.181), Fitzgerald and Speck (1945, p.22) and Gibson (1971, p.80) that the 1941 Stock Exchange listing requirements were an important factor in securing consolidated statements from New South Wales holding companies prior to 1962 - particularly for newly listed companies.

As was the case in N.S.W. it is apparent that a proportion of Victorian holding companies were consolidating prior to the first requirement to do so - up to approximately 14 percent in 1938. In fact 6 separate companies consolidated at one time or another over the period 1931-1938.

The provisions of the Victorian Act became operative in December 1938. In the year following the number of companies consolidating quadrupled (6 to 25). However, there was also a substantial rate of non-compliance with the Act (approximately 60 percent).[14] In spite of this a comparison of the Victorian experience immediately following the Act (1939 and 1940) with that in N.S.W. suggests that this Act was at least partially responsible for the marked increase in the number of Victorian consolidators.

The relatively high rate of non-compliance with the 1938 Victorian Act in its early years is a little surprising. The explanation may lie in the fact that the Act came into operation at the commencement of World War II - a time during which the matter of compliance or non-compliance with a financial reporting

---

14. Recall the Act provided for separate subsidiary accounts or consolidated accounts; yet the Table reveals no significant increase in the former type of disclosure in the post-Act period.

requirement may have been of relatively little importance and/or the accounting expertise (manpower) necessary to perform the task was simply not available. The absence of any formal monitoring and enforcement mechanism (possibly for similar reasons) might also be part of the explanation. The loss of trained staff during the War may also have resulted in Jobson's becoming (for a time at least) less efficient at reviewing and reproducing company accounts. In any event this rate of non-compliance had fallen substantially by 1953 (to approximately 19 percent), while in N.S.W. it remained at a relatively high 40 percent - a point to which we return in Chapter 3.1.

Table 2.1 allows one further observation. By 1940 forms of disclosure regarding subsidiaries, other than consolidation, had largely fallen into disuse. The option contained in both the Victorian Act, 1938 and the Sydney and Melbourne Stock Exchange listing requirements of 1941 appears to have been one that thereafter was very seldom exercised.[15] Appendix I indicates that over the decade there were only two instances of a company once

---

15. Perhaps because there was little support among practising accountants for this method. The technical/professional literature at this time reflects considerable concern over which of these methods would be most suitable. As early as 1928 Nixon (1928, p.364) had commented on the "impracticality" of separate subsidiary disclosures when the number of subsidiaries was large - an argument reinforced in Ferguson (1931), Fitzgerald (1938), Fitzgerald (1939) and Irish (1943). The charge of impracticality covered many sins including the arguments that such statements would be "costly", "confusing" (particularly in light of the lack of inter-company adjustments) and that they could result in "information overload" for shareholders or in "giving too much information away to one's competitors". Ferguson (1931, p.200) observes that this method was used in cases where there were only two or three subsidiaries. In the present study the maximum number of subsidiaries for which separate accounts were presented was three - most often it was one.

having adopted consolidated reporting switching back to a less extensive form of disclosure.[16] In one instance the subsidiaries had ceased to exist (Lincoln Mills (Australia) Ltd), in the other the subsidiaries remained and the change occurred without explanation.

To this point 4 N.S.W. and 6 Victorian companies have been identified as consolidating prior to the existence of any specific institutional requirement for them to do so.[17] Yet there is still another sample of companies that may be said to have voluntarily consolidated. Recalling that the listing requirements did not (until 1954) apply retrospectively, N.S.W. companies that were listed prior to 1941 and which did not subsequent to 1941 either reorganize and apply for relisting in Sydney, or apply for concurrent listing in Melbourne, may be described as being exempt from any specific requirement to consolidate - despite the fact that such requirements clearly existed. Note that the selection criteria minimize the potential effect of the concurrent consolidation requirements. The requirement that these companies be N.S.W. registered (i.e., incorporated) and only Sydney listed means that these companies are less likely to have an interstate/national operations base than those with multiple listings and are therefore less likely to be subject to the variety of implicit pressures to consolidate

---

16. While it is not ascertainable from Appendix I this statement holds true for the entire 1930-1962 period.

17. A detailed case history of each of these early "voluntary" consolidators is contained in Appendix II - which is intended to constitute evidence in support of the hypotheses developed in Chapter 4. Discussion of these case histories is deferred until Chapter 6.

that might exist for a company that, for example, conducted a large part of its operations in Victoria. It also means that these companies are not covered by any legislative consolidation requirements that might exist in other States. Similarly, the requirement that they have not reorganized and applied for relisting in Sydney, or applied for concurrent listing in Melbourne, means that they are technically not covered by any Stock Exchange requirement to consolidate.

The starting point for identifying this sample of voluntary consolidators was the Sydney Stock Exchange List as of January, 1941. All non-NSW registered companies were subsequently deleted, as were NSW registered companies that either applied for listing on the Melbourne Stock Exchange at any time before July, 1962 or were reorganized and applied for relisting in Sydney at any time after 1941. In order to establish the existence or otherwise of subsidiaries it was necessary to peruse each of the remaining company's accounts for each of the 22 years of interest (recall that the 1936 NSW Companies Act required the separate disclosure of "investments in subsidiaries").

In this manner it was possible to identify 74 companies that reported the existence of subsidiaries at some time between 1941-1962. Of these 74 companies, 44 (59 percent) decided to consolidate for the first time.

2.4 SUMMARY

Using the selection criteria identified in section 2.2 it has been possible to identify a number of companies that can be described as consolidating in the absence of any specific institutional requirement that may have compelled them to do so. These companies fall into three categories and may be described as:

- those that consolidated in Victoria prior to December, 1938;
- those that consolidated in N.S.W. prior to June, 1941; and
- those that consolidated in N.S.W. subsequent to June, 1941; but which were listed prior to this date and did not subsequently reorganize and apply for relisting in Sydney or apply for concurrent listing in Melbourne.

The number of companies identified from Jobson's Investment Digest in each of these samples was respectively, 4, 6 and 44. These companies comprise the basic data base for the empirical work which follows. The reasons why these particular companies chose to consolidate are the concern of Chapter 4.

CHAPTER 3

DEVELOPMENT OF AUSTRALIAN CAPITAL MARKETS : 1930-1960

Chapter 2 traces the evolution of consolidated financial reporting in Australia and presents evidence which, on the surface at least, appears to be consistent with the views of numerous authors (refer Chapter 2.3 supra) that the Stock Exchange listing requirements were an important factor in securing consolidated statements from companies prior to the legislative requirements.

This chapter briefly traces the evolution of Australian capital markets and particularly the market for debt capital. In so doing it demonstrates an association between developments in these markets (other than Stock Exchange requirements) and the widespread adoption of consolidated financial reporting. However, association is not causation and the articulation of possible cause and effect links is the concern of Chapter 4.

3.1 STOCK EXCHANGE REQUIREMENTS REVISITED

In contrast to Victoria the practice of consolidation in N.S.W. was essentially unregulated between 1940 and 1962. The only consolidation requirement was that contained in the 1941 revision of the Official List Requirements and, as observed in Chapter 2.3, the influence of this regulation appears to have been restricted to newly listed companies.

Nevertheless Ewart (1948), Fitzgerald (1944), Fitzgerald and Speck (1945) and Gibson (1971) all argue that the 1941 Stock Exchange listing requirements were an important factor in securing consolidated statements from New South Wales holding companies prior to 1962. At first glance the gradual increase in the proportion of holding companies consolidating in N.S.W. (indicated in Table 2.1) appears to be consistent with this view. However, on closer inspection there are a number of puzzling features in the data.

It was not until 1947 that there was any real increase in the number of holding companies consolidating in N.S.W. and it was not until 1953 that consolidation could really be described as commonplace. Even then the Editor of Jobson's remarked (January 29, 1953, p.7):

> [The regulations] are being honoured in many cases more in the breach than in the observance, and on the face of it, little, if anything, is being done to enforce the disclosure of information which the [Stock Exchange] regulations and the Acts require ... the failure of many companies to publish consolidated accounts of parent and subsidiaries is something which demands immediate action by the Stock Exchanges.

The relatively high non-compliance rates in N.S.W. (cf., Victoria) makes it unlikely that the Stock Exchange requirements were the principal cause of the spread of the consolidation phenomenon. Undoubtedly they had some effect. The jump in the proportion of consolidators between 1943 and 1950 from 6 to 32 percent is certainly consistent with the view that the September 1946 amendments had an impact - though primarily on newly listed companies. Recall that it was not until 1946 that companies applying for listing were actually required to enter into a "form of agreement" to abide by the listing requirements.

However, the doubling in the number of consolidators between 1950 and 1953 is unaccompanied by either a change in listing requirements or a doubling in the number of holding companies seeking listing over this period.[1] This observation and the still high non-compliance rate (40 percent) suggest an alternative explanation is required. The explanation pursued here is that the rapid spread of this form of reporting in the early 1950s was caused by developments in the external capital markets and, in particular, the market for debt.

3.2 SOURCES OF CAPITAL FOR AUSTRALIAN FIRMS

Over the thirty year time period of this study the Australian economy, and Australian firms, passed through a number of relatively distinct phases - in terms of both the level of economic activity and the relative degrees of reliance on alternative sources of funds to finance this activity. For present purposes the entire time period can be somewhat arbitrarily partitioned into a number of distinct sub-periods as indicated in Table 3.1.

Table 3.1

Level of Economic Activity: 1930 - 1960
By Sub-period

Time Period	Phase of Activity
1930 - 1934	Depression
1935 - 1940	Recovery
1941 - 1946	World War II
1947 - 1951	Rapid Growth
1952 - 1953	Recession
1954 - 1960	Growth

1. Table 7.4 infra indicates a 36 percent increase in the number of N.S.W. and Victorian registered holding companies between 1940 and 1950.

Statistics on the sources and uses of funds for the pre-war period are available in McGee (1927), and Keown (1954); for the post-war period in Keown (1952, 1954), Hall (1956), and Mathews and Harcourt (1964).[2] Documentation for the former period is less complete than for the latter. All authors relied on balance sheet data for public companies[3] listed on either the Sydney, Melbourne (or both) Stock Exchanges and the sample sizes ranged from 72 to 619 companies. Keown's (1954) time-series survey of the changes in sources of finance for a sample of 72 Australian public companies during the 1935 - 53 period is particularly relevant and is summarized, by sub-period, in Table 3.2.

From McGee (1927) and Keown (1952) it is possible to ascertain that following the depression there was a marked shift away from reliance on interest bearing, long-term finance (15 to 4 percent) to shorter term finance such as that provided by trade creditors (17 to 28 percent). Such interest bearing debt as was taken on was largely in the form of bank overdrafts (3 to 6-12

---

2. See also Mathews (1954), Chambers (1954) and Yorston (1956) - though the latter relies on secondary sources.

3. As reported in <u>Jobson's Investment Digest</u> or in the companies annual reports contained in Stock Exchange Files.

Table 3.2

Percentage Change in Sources of Funds
1935 - 1953

Source of Funds	1935-40	1941-46	1947-53
Shareholders' Funds			
Share issues (including premium)	30	15	18
Undistributed profits (including depreciation)	27	43	27
Sub-total	57	58	45
Trade creditors Other short-term creditors	36	53	37
Overdraft	5	(3)	5
Mortgages Debentures/Notes	2	(8)	13
Sub-total	43	42	55
Total	100	100	100

percent.[4] The percentage of expansion financed by these sources of funds is shown in the first column of Table 3.2.

The onset of World War II was accompanied by the introduction of "Capital Issues Controls".[5] The effect of these controls is apparent in column 2 of Table 3.2. During the 1941 - 46 period the percentage change in funds raised by share issues fell from 30 to 15 percent. There were also net debt retirements. This fact and the capital issues controls imply that such expansion as occurred appears to have been largely financed through retained earnings and trade credit.

Capital issues controls were not abandoned until December 1953 although following the war they seem to have fallen most heavily on fixed interest securities (debentures, notes and preference shares) with the Capital Issues Committee pegging the rates at which industrial companies could borrow in order to reduce competition with Government borrowings (Henderson, 1954). Over this same period the central bank had been concerned to

---

4. In principle such advances have always been repayable on demand, in practice many companies remained indefinitely in overdraft. Evidence on this practice appears in the 1937 Royal Commission on Banking. For example, at p.90 the Superintendent of the Bank of Australasia states:

> Overdrafts are not granted for definite periods and are repayable on demand. In practice, however, the majority of overdrafts, particularly those against the security of landed property are allowed to continue for long periods and repayment is sought only in exceptional circumstances.

A similar statement is made on p.517 by the Assistant General Manager of the Bank of Adelaide.

5. The controls applied to all "capital issues" for purposes deemed "non-essential" - including debentures and notes (Henderson, 1954).

reduce the demand for bank facilities and directed that commercial bank overdrafts should be limited to the short-term needs of business and not used in cases where the real need was for long-term debt capital (McInnes, 1954; Hirst, 1964).[6] Under these conditions Life Assurance Offices and Trustee companies became important sources of long-term (mortgage) finance (Hall, 1956).[7] Indeed, from Keown (1952) and Hall (1956) it is possible to ascertain that between 1950 and 1954 overdrafts had fallen from an average of around 9 to 0 percent of funds supplied and mortgages had increased from around 4 to 8 percent. Over the same period reliance on debentures and notes increased from an average of 0 to 9 percent of funds.

Despite the capital issues controls the period 1947-51 was one of rapid growth for the corporate sector which peaked in mid-1951 and the years 1950-51 saw boom conditions in new issue markets, the evolution of the short-term money market (pioneered by the finance companies) and the innovation of the registered unsecured note (McInnes, 1954; Grimwood, 1960). Indeed, the statistics in Keown (1952) and Hall (1956) allow the inferences that between 1950 and 1952 the average proportion of long-term interest bearing debt (including overdrafts) in firms' capital structures had risen from 10 to 20 percent; a substantial

---

6. It was not until 1962 that "fixed" or "term" lending by the Australian trading banks evolved and while the banks would provide mortgage loans generally speaking they preferred to lend "short" (Hirst, 1964).

7. Between 1930 and 1960 (and to an extent even today) such companies had a settled policy of lending only on the security of a first mortgage on real estate, and then, on only a modest portion of the current value of the mortgaged asset (Gole, 1970).

component of this increase was a result of the public placement of funds, and that by 1953 the average aggregate debt-equity ratio for the first time exceeded 1:1. The increasing importance of the debt market is also evident in column 3 of Table 3.2.

Between mid-1951 and mid-1953 the economy was in recession - an impropitious time for fund raising. However by the end of this brief period relaxation of the restrictions on bank lending, the removal of capital issues controls and a reduction in corporate tax rates had set the foundations for another period of sustained growth. Indeed it was during the 1953-60 period that the long term debt markets, and in particular the market for public debt, can be said to have really developed. For example, debenture/note issues represented only 30 percent of the new monies raised by listed companies in 1955; by 1960 they represented 80 percent (Grimwood, 1960; Mathews, 1964; Fitzgerald, 1965).[8]

In summary the post-depression period may be characterized as one of low reliance on debt relative to earlier times; and one in which the principal source of long-term debt was on overdraft facility with a trading bank. This position remained essentially unchanged until the end of World War II. In the expansionary years that followed the large institutional lenders (insurance and trustee companies) came to play an important part in the long-term, fixed interest capital market. It was not until the decade of the fifties that the public became an important direct source

8. Similarly, in January 1950 there were only 12 debenture issues listed on the Sydney Stock Exchange (excluding banks). By 1960 there were 26; though there were also some 50 companies with unsecured notes on issue. There were also many companies (e.g., finance companies) with unlisted public debt.

of this form of capital.

3.3 IMPLICATIONS FOR THE EVOLUTION OF CONSOLIDATED REPORTING

The preceding discussion indicates that the decade of the 1950s commenced with a fundamental restructuring in the nature of corporate capital markets in Australia. An increasing reliance on debt as compared to equity capital and, in particular, on publicly-placed compared to privately-placed debt was accompanied by a number of financial innovations, including the registered unsecured note and the convertible note.

As observed above, prior to December 1953 the Government, through the Capital Issues Committee, controlled and monitored the level of listed public companies debt. As a consequence this matter would be less likely to be one requiring the detailed attention of parties contracting with the firm. It is argued here that the removal of Governmental controls would create a need for private or contractual restrictions on leverage. The monitoring of compliance with such restrictions, particularly in what might be described as "group lending" situations (i.e., lending to a company or companies that stand in a parent/subsidiary relation with one another) would require information of a type not available in conventional parent company accounts - that is, information on "group" leverage, etc. This argument is pursued in depth in the next chapter.

The preceding discussion foreshadows hypotheses about the relationship between debt contracting practices and the adoption of consolidated reporting. To illustrate this point Exhibit I reproduces extracts from the "Deed Polls" supporting the first (so

EXHIBIT 1
DEED POLL EXTRACTS

The Myer Emporium Limited

3 (a) Until such time as all of the Notes shall have been either surrendered to the Company or redeemed by it the Company shall not borrow or permit any of its subsidiaries to borrow any sum which will result in (i) The aggregate borrowing by the Company and its subsidiaries both secured and unsecured at any time exceeding the amount of the net tangible assets of the Company and its subsidiaries (as disclosed in the latest **consolidated balance sheet of the Company and its subsidiaries** published by the Company prior to that time); or (ii) The aggregate secured borrowings of the Company and its subsidiaries exceeding three-fourths of such amount of the net tangible assets.

(b) The Company shall not create or issue any unsecured loan stock or Notes ranking in priority to the Notes but subject to paragraph (a) of this Condition, it may create and issue further unsecured Notes ranking **pari passu** with this issue.
[Registered Unsecured Note Prospectus, 17 November 1950, Emphasis Added]

Henry Berry & Company (Australasia) Limited

6 (a) The total borrowings of **the Company and its Subsidiaries** are limited to £1,250,000;

(b) The total secured borrowings of **the Company and its Subsidiaries** from any Banks are limited to £500,000;

(c) The Company may not issue any unsecured Loan Stock or Notes ranking in priority to or **pari passu** with the issue of these Notes;

(d) The Company and its Subsidiaries may not issue Debentures Debenture Stock Mortgages or other Charges over their assets excepting -

(i) Security to a Bank within the limits of Clause 6 (b);

(ii) An issue of Debentures for a sum not exceeding £64,500 to rank **pari passu** with the Company's existing issue of Debentures amounting to £135,500.

(iii) An issue of Debentures or Debenture Stock for a sum not exceeding £200,000 upon or after the redemption of the existing Debentures including any issue within the terms of the previous sub-clause.

[Convertible Unsecured Note Prospectus, 30 September 1950; Emphasis Added]

far as can be ascertained) listed registered unsecured note and the first listed convertible unsecured note offerred to the Australian public. In both cases these innovative financial instruments placed restrictions on the borrowings of the company and its subsidiaries. In the former the limitation was explicitly defined over the consolidated balance sheet of the company and the subsidiaries. In the latter a consolidation is implied since presumably inter-company borrowings would be excluded from the absolute limitations on debt i.e., inter-company (consolidation) adjustments would be required to determine compliance with this covenant. The preceding discussion also implies that the hypothesized relationship may be time dependent. That is debt related variables can be expected to be more significant in periods in which there are no Government controls than in those in which there are.

3.4 SUMMARY

The evidence presented in this Chapter indicates that the rapid spread of consolidated financial reporting in an essentially unregulated environment (N.S.W.) coincided with the removal of Capital Issues Controls and the development of a market for public debt. The argument also suggests a three-way partitioning of the samples of consolidators identified in Chapter 2 i.e., those that consolidated prior to, during and subsequent to the period Capital Issues Controls were effectively in place.

CHAPTER 4

HYPOTHESIS DEVELOPMENT

Taken together Chapters 2 and 3 reveal a strong association between the widespread adoption of consolidated financial reporting, the removal of capital issues controls and the development of a market for public debt. Chapter 3 also argues that this relationship is more than coincidental. That conjecture is pursued here.

The central argument is that consolidation is a manifestation of contracting procedures aimed at firm value maximization by preventing (or making easier to detect) opportunistic behaviour by managers rather than being the result of opportunistic behaviour per se. With one exception (Zimmer, 1986) existing studies of management's policy choices have relied on the latter assumption. The distinction is important, for as Zimmer (1986, pp.1-2) observes it provides a richer description of the accounting choice setting and in so doing can be used to explain why leverage and accounting method choice might be related (even in the absence of bond covenants) or why large firms do not always choose income reducing accounting techniques (as predicted by a "political cost" hypothesis)[1].

---

1. Zimmer (1986) studied accounting for interest by Australian real estate developers. The basic argument is that contracts negotiated between developers and customers, lenders and/or coventurers require the capitalization of interest under certain conditions i.e., either when interest payments result in increases in the firm's revenue or when capitalization minimizes monitoring costs.

The chapter is structured as follows. The nature of the contracting problems confronting managers and suppliers of debt and equity capital are considered in sections 4.1 and 4.2 respectively. In both cases what appear to be ex ante least cost solutions to these contracting problems imply that consolidated financial reporting will be required to monitor compliance with, and performance under, the agreement. Section 4.3 factors the costs of consolidation into the analysis. These three sections lead to a number of hypotheses about the attributes of firms that consolidate. Section 4.4 considers the (conventional) alternative explanation that management's choice of accounting method (i.e., consolidation) is a result of opportunistic action taken after contracts are put in place. Section 4.4 briefly summarizes the argument developed in this chapter.

4.1 INCENTIVE PROBLEMS AND CONTRACTING SOLUTIONS CONFRONTING MANAGEMENT AND SUPPLIERS OF DEBT CAPITAL

With risky debt outstanding management, acting in the shareholders' interests, has incentives to design a firm's operating characteristics and financial structure in ways which benefit shareholders to the detriment of debtholders. Smith and Warner (1979, p.118-119) identify four principal sources of this conflict; dividends, asset substitution, underinvestment and claim dilution.[2] For ease of exposition attention is directed primarily at the latter. However analogous arguments could be made in

---

2. The categories are neither mutually exclusive nor exhaustive. For example, perquisite consumption, bankruptcy and information asymmetry may also constitute agency costs of debt.

respect of each of these sources of conflict.

The problem of claim dilution is usually portrayed in the following way. If a firm sells debt and the debt is priced assuming that no additional debt will be issued the value of the debtholder's claims is reduced by issuing claims of the same or higher priority. Both Smith and Warner (1979, p.136) and Whittred and Zimmer (1985, p.5) observe that shareholders' actions of this type are typically limited by either a restriction or prohibition on the issue of claims of higher priority, or through a requirement that existing debt be upgraded to the same priority as the proposed debt.[3] There are, of course, other ways in which debtholders' claims can be diluted; particularly in group lending contexts. The assumption of quasi-debt by a borrowing corporation (e.g., guarantees of the indebtedness of a related company), the transfer of assets to related corporations not subject to the initial debt agreement and at other than arm's length (market) prices, or the issue of debt by subsidiary corporations all serve to reduce the coverage afforded the debtholders of the parent company.

In Australian debt contracts the assumption of quasi-debt is at least partially controlled by the way in which the restriction on total liabilities is defined. Total liabilities are typically restricted to a percentage (between 60 and 80) of total tangible assets. Liabilities are specifically defined to include any

---

3. These authors survey debt contracting practices in the U.S. and Australia respectively. They also report that the contracts typically restrict the total amount of all debt that can be issued.

contingent liabilities of the borrowing firm (Whittred and Zimmer, 1985, p.4-5). Similarly, the issue of debt by subsidiary corporations is controlled by defining the borrowing limitations over the companies in the "group"[4]. The problem of controlling non-arm's length exchanges (at artificial prices) is more complicated and is considered separately below.

Claim dilution through non-arm's length transactions can be controlled in a number of ways. A complete prohibition on transactions between related corporations, or alternatively, allowing bondholders the right to veto any such transactions are both possible, though impractical, since they presumably defeat the purpose of being related companies. Since the problem is basically that assets in the borrowing company can be transferred to a related company not subject to the initial debt agreement, the solution would appear to be to restore access to these assets in the event of default. This can be achieved in either of two non-mutually exclusive ways. The borrowing corporation could provide a charge (fixed, floating or some combination of the two)

4. Strictly, the borrowing corporation and its guarantors. This point resurfaces subsequently.

over its assets including "shares in subsidiaries".[5] Alternatively, it could have the related (subsidiary) corporations guarantee the debt.

In the event that, at maturity, there are insufficient assets to satisfy the debt the former strategy provides creditors with two options. They may either sell the "shares in subsidiaries" or they may force the subsidiaries into liquidation in order to gain access to their assets (strictly, the proceeds from disposal of those assets). Not only is the latter process time consuming and costly, but in the process the creditors of the initial borrowing corporation stand as residual equity holders in, not creditors of, the subsidiaries (i.e., they lose priority). This indirect access to subsidiary company assets can in large part be avoided by having the subsidiaries joined as guarantors. In the event of default the creditors proceed directly to the guarantors for satisfaction of the debt. In the legal processes that ensue they would stand as unsecured creditors in the guarantor and thereby retain some priority over the residual equity holders of the guarantor. Of course this process is itself costly and, other

5. The most common form of security for bank accommodation (i.e., overdrafts) to joint stock companies was (and remains) the equitable mortgage or mortgage debenture (Porter 1970). An equitable, as distinct from a legal, mortgage merely creates a registerable charge upon property, it does not vest legal ownership in the mortgagee. An equitable mortgage comprises both a fixed and a floating charge. The former attaches essentially to "fixed assets" - land, freeholds, plant, machinery and equipment - often in the form of a legal mortgage. Unlike the fixed charge, the floating charge does not restrain the company from dealing with the assets covered by the charge in the normal course of its business; at least, not until such time as an event occurs which crystallizes the charge. The most common form of security supporting debentures or notes is a floating charge over all of the assets of the borrowing corporation (Armitage, 1981).

things equal, a secured creditor of the borrowing corporation would prefer to stand as a secured creditor in the guarantors. This can be achieved by having the guarantees supported by a charge over the guarantor's assets which provides direct access to those assets in the event the charge crystallizes.[6]

Note also that creditors are unlikely to be indifferent to the manner in which these guarantees are effected. Ceteris paribus a rational creditor will prefer more guarantees to less (i.e., guarantees from as many as possible of the related corporations). Further, creditors will prefer that the guarantors be jointly <u>and</u> severally liable rather than jointly <u>or</u> severally liable.[7] The former strategy provides creditors with maximum flexibility if legal proceedings are necessary. A creditor may proceed against any, or all, of the guarantors for the entire debt and in any order. This is not possible under either joint or several liability (refer Farquharson, 1956, p.21). Finally, as was

---

6. Whittred's (1983) survey of the pro-forma lending agreements written by all Australian trading banks and a number of the leading institutional lenders (insurance companies) indicates that it is usual for both a floating charge over the shares in subsidiaries and guarantees from subsidiaries to be effected. Further, the guarantees are often supported by a floating charge over the assets of the guarantor. As discussed above, the combination of the floating charge over shares in subsidiaries and the cross-guarantees provides creditors with a greater number of options (ways out) in the event of default - thus their combined use is not surprising. Since either strategy provides creditors with access to guarantors assets there can be little difference to management in the cost of providing either or both. However, there are potential benefits which can be characterized as an increase in the issue price of the claim.

7. That is, joint <u>and</u> several liability provides creditors with a portfolio of options which, following Merton (1973), will be more valuable than the option provided by either joint <u>or</u> several liability alone.

argued above, creditors will prefer that the guarantees be supported by a charge over the assets of the guarantors (refer also to footnote 6).

Thus, a charge over shares in subsidiaries, or more particularly the effecting of a set of cross-guarantees is a way of increasing the probability that either at maturity, or in the event of default, the value of the assets available for satisfaction of the debt exceeds the promised repayment. To put it another way, cross-guarantees help to "undo" the effects of limited liability on creditors and in doing so create a demand for a set of financial statements that, likewise, undoes the effects of separately incorporated companies within a group.

Evidence consistent with these arguments is contained in the Whittred's (1983) survey where it is reported that when a borrowing application covers a group of companies bankers invariably require a set of cross-guarantees - and from as many members of the group as possible. The guarantees provide, as a matter of form, for the guarantor's liability to be joint and several. It is also standard for the individual guarantees to be supported by a charge (equitable mortgage) over each company's assets. Further, in such circumstances bank standing instructions usually require:

> Where an application covers the borrowing of a group of companies, balance sheet and trading statements need not be submitted for each individual borrowing/ guaranteeing company (subject to other requirements of State Administration) provided advances are covered by a full set of cross guarantees supported by mortgage debentures from each company. In such cases, it will suffice if the following are furnished:
>
> - Balance Sheet and Trading and Profit and Loss Statement of the parent company; and

> - **Consolidated Balance Sheet and Trading and Profit and Loss Statement of the group excluding all inter-company items.**
>
> However, the relative details applicable to the other borrowing/guaranteeing companies in the group should be on record at the branch and any material adverse trend in trading results by any of the companies in the group commented upon in "General Remarks".
>
> Branches must at all times satisfy themselves by proper examination and comparison that the consolidated accounts cover only these companies from which cross guarantees and mortgage debentures are held.[8]
>
> (emphasis added)

Together with Exhibit 1 in Chapter 3.3 these observations support the proposition that cross-guarantees either implicitly or explicitly generate a demand for consolidated financial statements.

Similarly, a set of cross-guarantees implies that any constraints placed upon management's behaviour (e.g., borrowing limitations) will be defined relative to the financial position and performance of the group - defined as the borrowing corporation and its guarantors - and not just the borrowing corporation; thus reinforcing this demand. Whittred and Zimmer's (1985) survey of the trust deeds supporting Australian debenture and note issues supports this view. In each instance in which cross-guarantees were present such borrowing or liability limitations as were included in the contract were defined over a consolidation of the borrowing company and its guarantors.

---

8. This quote is taken from the standing instructions of one of the banks referred to in footnote 6. It was possible to ascertain that this (or a similar) provision exists in each of the Australian trading banks.

The arguments to this point are summarized in Figure 4.1. As can be seen the circumstances in which cross-guarantees are likely to be found assume considerable importance; for once they have been identified, so to have the conditions under which consolidation is likely to occur.

Subject to the well established legal principle that the directors of a company must exercise their powers for the benefit of the company,[9] the extent of inter-company guarantees is likely to depend largely on the degree of ownership of the related corporations and the extent to which the proposed debt is supported by the assets-in-place.[10] The former variable relates largely to the costs of effecting cross-guarantees, the latter to the potential benefits, in the manner discussed below.

By effecting a set of cross-guarantees management changes (increases) the probability and hence the expected value of the pay-off in certain states of nature. In particular, the guarantees are designed to ensure that in the event of default, the value of the assets available for satisfaction of the debt (V_A) are greater than they otherwise would have been - thereby minimizing the extent of creditor losses or claim dilution. The

---

9. Refer Nash (1984, p.571), Richard Brady Franks Ltd V. Price (1937) 58 CLR 112, p.135 and Gower (1969, Chapter 23).

10. The term is used in the Myers (1977) sense of the word. Myers conceptualizes the value of the firm as comprising the value of "assets-in-place" and the value of "growth options". The principal distinction between the two classes of assets is that the value of the latter depends on future discretionary expenditures by the firm (p.155). The assets that may be collateralized (i.e., legal mortgage), or in some other way (i.e., equitable mortgage, deed, guarantee), made available for the satisfaction of a debt may be regarded as a subset of those "in-place".

FIGURE 4.1

Monitoring Implications of Debt Contracting in Group Contexts

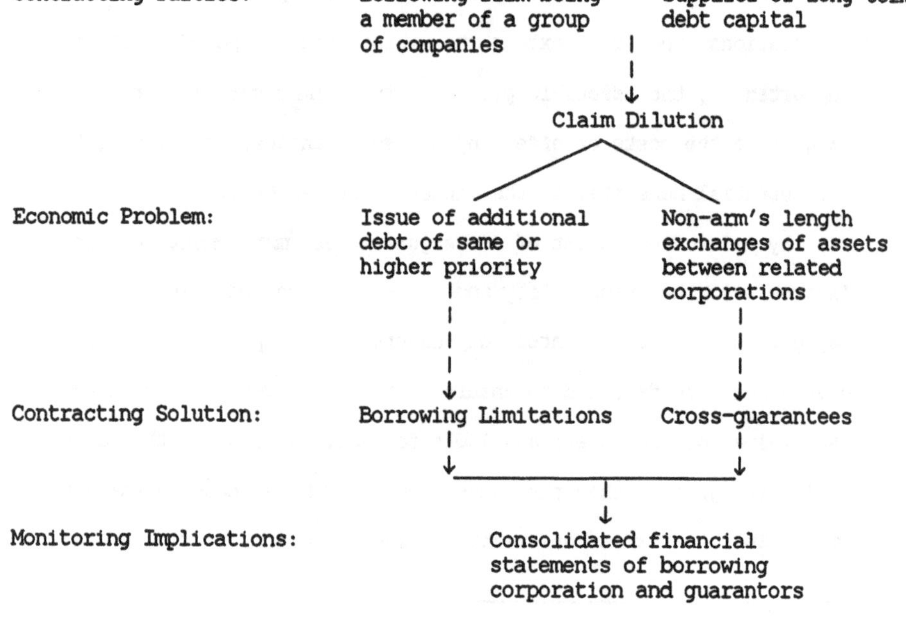

potential benefits to management include any or all of the following - a reduction in interest rate, an increase in time to maturity, a less restrictive set of covenants or, following Myers (1977), an increase in debt capacity (the amount borrowed or capable of being borrowed). If default risk increases in the ratio of debt (X) to the security offered for the debt (V_A) then the potential benefits of a set of cross-guarantees will also increase in X/V_A. The costs to management include the negotiation and legal costs associated with effecting the guarantees. If the related corporations are wholly-owned these costs are likely to be relatively low. If they are less than wholly-owned then the costs include any costs arising out of potential legal actions for fraud on, or oppression of, the minority.[11] This analysis of the relative costs and benefits of effecting a set of cross-guarantees indicates that they are most likely to be found:

(a) between a parent and its wholly-owned subsidiaries,

(b) when the ratio of the proposed debt to the assets available for satisfaction of the debt (i.e., assets-in-place) is relatively high.

In summary, the preceding arguments imply that under certain conditions (i.e., the presence of cross-guarantees) management has an incentive to supply a set of financial statements defined over the assets and liabilities of the borrowing corporation and its

11. The actions which might constitute fraud on, or oppression of, the minority and potential sources of relief are discussed in Gower (1969, pp.564-578 and pp.595-604) respectively.

guarantors that adjusts for any inter-company dependencies.[12] Thus it is hypothesized that:

> H1: In the presence of a set of cross-guarantees management is more likely to supply a consolidation of the borrowing corporation and its guarantors for monitoring purposes.

There are two things to note about these financial statements. First, they are a "consolidation" of the borrowing company and its guarantors and they differ in this respect from those prepared under generally accepted accounting principles, where the usual area of consolidation is the company and its subsidiaries. Second, the statements are prepared under the provisions of a private contracting arrangement. There is usually no requirement that they be made public or that they correspond with the financial statements adopted for external reporting purposes. However, they would do so if all subsidiaries are guarantors and/or if there exists in the debt contract a specific requirement for a consolidation of the borrowing corporation and its subsidiaries as well as one of the borrowing corporation and its guarantors.[13]

4.2 INCENTIVE PROBLEMS AND CONTRACTING SOLUTIONS CONFRONTING MANAGEMENT AND SUPPLIERS OF EQUITY CAPITAL

In much the same way as debt contracts in group lending contexts may incorporate, explicitly or implicitly, a

---

12. Note that creditors are unlikely to be indifferent to the definitions employed in these financial statements or the nature of the adjustments to be made (refer Leftwich, 1983; Whittred and Zimmer, 1985).

13. Whittred and Zimmer (1985, footnote 12) reveal that the trust deeds supporting listed debentures and notes invariably specify the latter.

consolidation requirement those written between shareholders and management may also. In this regard the principal contracts of interest are the Articles of Association and the management compensation plan (if any).

Consider the latter first. Envisage a world in which shareholders have rational (but not necessarily homogeneous) expectations, capital markets are efficient, and take the case of a single firm, owner-managed, desirous of raising additional (external) equity finance. Assume also that this initial owner has elected to stay on in the capacity of manager. Then among other things the new owner(s) will want to agree upon some basis of rewarding the old owner in his capacity as a manager (with a costly to observe marginal product) rather than as a risk-bearer. Given the incentive problems that can arise in such circumstances it would not be surprising to see management's compensation linked directly to that of the remaining shareholders through, among other things, the use incentive compensation schemes defined over accounting based performance indicators such as net profit or rate of return i.e., external financial reports may facilitate performance evaluation (Watts, 1977; Smith and Watts, 1982).

Consider now a more complicated scenario, one in which a single owner/manager with a declining proportional equity investment elects to organise his activities through the medium of a number of closely related (subsidiary) companies and the shares in these subsidiaries constitute the principal asset of the parent company. In these circumstances the difficulties of evaluating managerial performance on the basis of parent company income or rate of return alone are obvious - particularly when the principal source of parent company income is inter-company dividends, the amount and timing of which are largely at management's discretion. What is required is a measure or index which reflects the performance of the entire group of companies for which management is primarily responsible - one which does not (a) double count the results of inter-company transactions and (b) is resilient to possible management manipulation of the type referred to above. Accounting performance measures with this property would be defined over a set of consolidated accounts.[14]

Apart from playing a role in the managerial incentive structure financial information may also be required for monitoring purposes. In the present case consider the difficulties of monitoring the consequences of any opportunistic behaviour by management in subsidiaries which appear in the parent company's accounts only in the aggregate figure "shares in subsidiaries". To the extent that such behaviour is shifted "off balance sheet" the parent company's financial statements become correspondingly less useful as a monitoring device. What mechanisms exist to overcome this problem? The first that comes to mind is the presentation of the separate accounts of the company and all of its subsidiaries. But consider the following additional complications. First, it is possible for subsidiaries to be set up in a form which exempts them from the usual reporting requirements attaching to public company status (e.g., exempt

14. Such an index would be "hard" in the Ijiri (1975) sense of the word. Case Study 6, Appendix 2 provides such an example.

proprietary companies).[15] Second, even if separate subsidiary accounts were to be made available through a private contracting arrangement their utility as a monitoring device would be limited if inter-company transactions of any frequency or magnitude take place. Of course, separate disclosure of the latter is always a possibility. The accounting technique of consolidation would, on the other hand, avoid or overcome these complications.

If, following Jensen and Meckling (1976, pp.346-347) and Watts (1977, p.59-60), it is accepted that the optimum level of monitoring increases as the owner/manager's fractional claim on the firm decreases;[16] and if for the reasons discussed above it is also accepted that consolidated financial statements are a more suitable means for monitoring either managerial performance or compliance with contractual restrictions (such as those discussed immediately below) in group contexts then it may be hypothesized that:

H2: The smaller is management's relative share of the parent company's equity the greater the likelihood that management will consolidate for external reporting purposes.

---

15. Fitzgerald (1938, p.139) observes that Australian holding companies relied heavily on proprietary company subsidiaries for which there was no legal obligation to publish accounts and Nixon (1928, p.363) had commented critically on this practice a decade earlier. Gibson (1967, p.585) argues that the proprietary company was employed:

> ...as a device to avoid the disclosure of the financial position of companies by transferring the operations and assets of public companies to subsidiaries which enjoyed the privileges of proprietary companies.

16. Because, it is argued, the marginal benefits to a monitoring induced reduction in management's opportunistic behaviour are increasing.

The argument to this point (summarized in Figure 4.2) has been that under certain conditions management is likely to contract, ex ante, in either the Articles of Association or a separate compensation agreement, for the provision of consolidated financial statements.

Figure 4.2

Monitoring Implications of Equity Contracting in Group Contexts

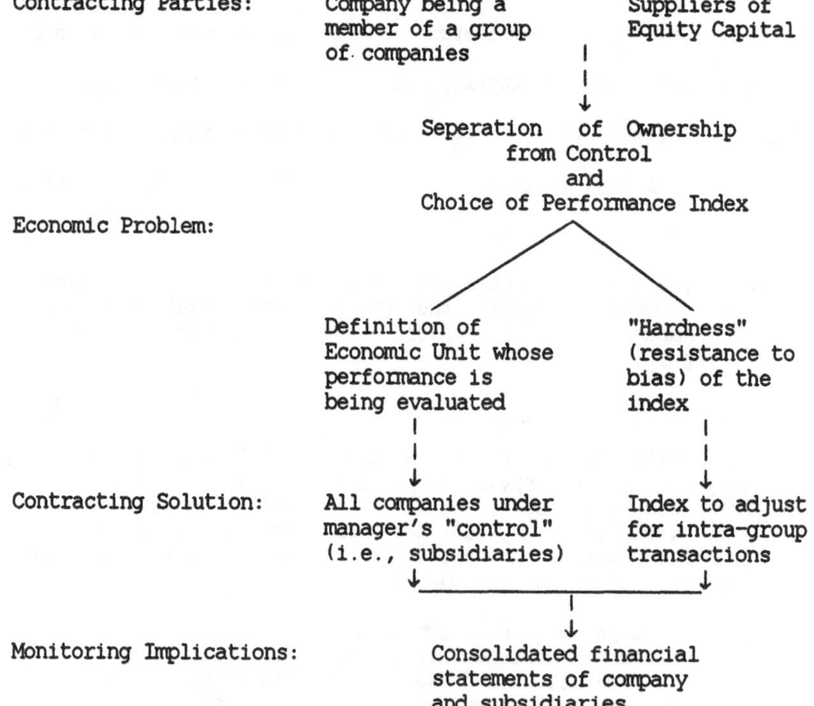

A company's Articles may also operate indirectly to provide an incentive for management to consolidate. For example, the Articles may contain borrowing restrictions similar to those contained in a company's debt contracts. There is an established (though old) case law on the interpretation of such restrictions[17] and the set of model articles (Schedule 2, Table A) contained in both the NSW and Victorian Companies Acts from 1936-1960 contained the following restriction (Article 69):

> The amount for the time being remaining undischarged of moneys borrowed or raised by the directors for the purposes of the company (otherwise than by the issue of share capital) shall not at any time exceed the issued share capital of the company without the sanction of the company in general meeting.

While this particular restriction does not provide any incentive to consolidate, it is possible that in more complex group situations such a restriction might be defined over group assets or equities thereby providing the appropriate incentive. Collins (1940, p.19) asserts that in the majority of cases companies adopted their own articles and specifically excluded the operation of Table A.[18] However, in the absence of any empirical evidence on this issue the possibility that a company's Articles contained a borrowing restriction which provided an incentive to consolidate must be allowed for.

---

17. Refer O'Dowd and Menzies (1940, p.742) and Spender and Wallace (1937, p.631).

18. Even if a company adopted its own articles the provisions of Table A operated to the extent that they were not inconsistent with the companies own articles; unless the operation of Table A was entirely excluded (Yorston and Fortescue, 1953, p.69).

Thus it may be also hypothesized that:

H3: Management is more likely to consolidate for external reporting purposes if

(a) the articles of association either specifically require them to do so or they contain certain kinds of borrowing restrictions; or

(b) there exists a compensation scheme which remunerates management on the basis of "group" performance.

4.3 THE DERIVED DEMAND FOR CONSOLIDATED FINANCIAL REPORTING

Management will contract to supply consolidated financial statements when the benefits from doing so exceed the costs. Sections 4.1 and 4.2 identify the conditions under which all contracting parties (i.e., management, shareholders and debtholders) could potentially benefit from consolidated financial statements. The benefits to these claimholders accrue in terms of the reduction in value loss (i.e., deadweight losses associated with opportunistic behaviour by management) that is occasioned by the improved monitoring facilities. Hence it is not surprising that the conditions identified in 4.1 and 4.2 may be characterised as potentially high agency cost situations. The benefits may be characterised as an increase in the issue price of the claims (a reduction in the required rate of return).[19] The costs include the costs of production (preparation, audit and printing) and distribution (mailing) of the financial reports. These costs are likely to behave in a relatively predictable manner across reporting alternatives.

---

19. This attribute is selected for the purpose of illustration only. In the case of debt there are a number of negotiable attributes besides price (e.g., security offerred and the amount and maturity of the loan) - see also section 4.1.

For example, under most reasonable scenarios parent company only statements would, relative to parent company and separate subsidiary accounts or a full consolidation, appear to be the least cost alternative. Similarly, provided each of the subsidiaries produces accounts, the parent plus separate subsidiary statements option would seem to have lower production, but higher distribution, costs than a full consolidation.[20] It also seems likely that the direct costs of consolidation including auditing costs, increase with a number of factors (e.g., the volume of inter-company transactions, the degree of ownership of subsidiaries, their geographical dispersion, the heterogeneity of their balance dates, the extent of cross-holdings and so on). Unfortunately it is not possible to collect data on these factors due to the nature of the disclosures made by Australian companies over the 1930-1962 period. However, it does seem likely that the greater the number of subsidiaries the greater the probability of any one or more of these complicating factors being present. Thus, this variable can be adopted as a proxy for the likely complexity, and therefore the costs, of consolidation.

Increasing costs <u>per se</u> provide an incentive not to consolidate. On the other hand, as the number of subsidiaries increases so too does the complexity of the monitoring problem and hence, the monitoring costs, for external claimholders. If these

---

20. If the subsidiaries were not required to produce accounts for public distribution (i.e., they were proprietary companies over the period of this study) there may also be indirect costs associated with anything other than parent company disclosures - for example, those costs associated with the revelation of previously undisclosed information regarding the financial position and performance of related corporations.

costs increase more rapidly than the costs of consolidation, and if management is forced to carry these costs because external claimholders price-protect then it will pay management to consolidate. Thus it is also hypothesized that:

H4: The greater the number of subsidiaries the greater the likelihood that management will consolidate for external reporting purposes.

4.4 EX POST OPPORTUNISTIC BEHAVIOUR

A basic premise in much of the existing accounting method choice literature is that changes in accounting method occur because the change allows management to avoid the costs associated with violating restrictive covenants or to expropriate the wealth of other claimholders in the firm. In the absence of contract details leverage is often used as a proxy for the "closeness" to these restrictive covenants.[21] Thus it is usually argued that:

Alternative H1: Firms that are close to their debt covenants are more likely to use income increasing (or leverage reducing) accounting methods than those which are not.

Analytically this hypothesis is not particularly compelling. The financial statement effects of consolidation are problematic. They may be leverage and income (and variance thereof) increasing or reducing depending on the facts of any particular case. Given that there is debt in the subsidiaries capital structure the nature of the consolidation process is such that the debt/equity ratio (in book terms) must always increase. Of course, debt/asset ratios need not. Empirically the results in Chapter 6.2 reveal that, on average, consolidation is income and leverage (debt/total

---

21. Holthausen and Leftwich (1983) review this literature.

tangible assets) increasing.

Note that while ex post opportunism is offerred as a plausable explanation for management's accounting choices it is not inconsistent with the ex ante arguments developed earlier. Indeed both factors could be operating. The question reduces to one regarding the relative significance of the factors and it is to this issue that attention is directed in Chapter 6. For the reasons discussed there this alternative hypothesis is ultimately rejected.

4.5 SUMMARY

Holding companies with risky debt outstanding or in which there is seperation of ownership from control of resources face potential problems (e.g., claim dilution, performance evaluation) the contracting solutions to which (e.g., cross-guarantees, index choice) either implicitly or explicitly require consolidated financial statements to be part of the contracting equilibrium. The manner in which the specific hypotheses developed here are tested is considered next.

CHAPTER 5

RESEARCH DESIGN CONSIDERATIONS

The analysis of Chapter 2 identifies three samples of firms that may be called voluntary consolidators. The arguments of Chapters 3 and 4 were directed at establishing the reason these companies adopted this more extensive and more costly form of financial reporting, particularly in the absence of institutional requirements for them to do so. This chapter considers the manner in which the hypotheses developed in Chapter 4 may be tested and describes the data collection procedures instituted.

5.1 RESEARCH DESIGN AND LIMITATIONS

The hypotheses developed in Chapter 4 fall into two basic sets - both pertaining to the underlying contractual structure of the firm. Hypothesis 1 is concerned with debt related incentives to consolidate, hypotheses 2 and 3 with equity related incentives. Hypothesis 4 is an attempt to factor the costs of the consolidation process into the analysis. In principle the effect of these variables should be observable as either a change in one or more of these factors prior to consolidation or as a systematic difference between those firms that consolidate at a point in time and those that do not.

The samples of companies identified in Chapter 2 fall into two basic sets - those 10 that consolidated prior to regulation and those 44 that consolidated after the introduction of the regulations but which were, technically, exempt from these regulations. For ease of reference Figure 5.1 summarizes these features of the data. The analysis of Chapter 3 suggests a finer

FIGURE 5.1

Treatment Sample: Voluntary Consolidators
By State and Time

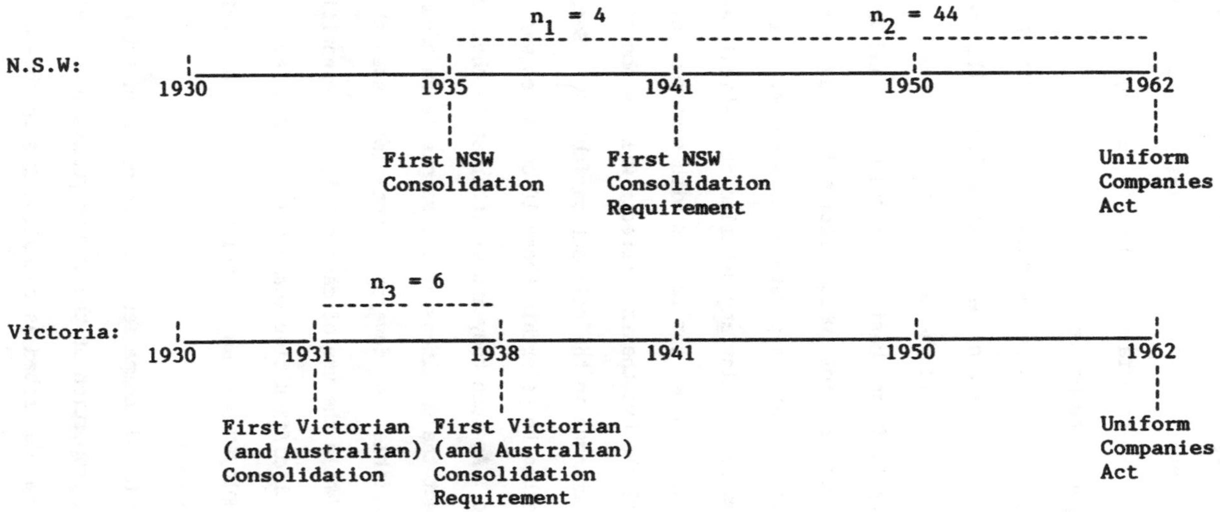

N.S.W:

1930 — 1935 — 1941 — 1950 — 1962

$n_1 = 4$ (1935–1941)

$n_2 = 44$ (1941–1962)

1935: First NSW Consolidation

1941: First NSW Consolidation Requirement

1962: Uniform Companies Act

Victoria:

1930 — 1931 — 1938 — 1941 — 1950 — 1962

$n_3 = 6$ (1931–1938)

1931: First Victorian (and Australian) Consolidation

1938: First Victorian (and Australian) Consolidation Requirement

1962: Uniform Companies Act

partitioning of the post-regulation consolidators. The argument in that Chapter implies that debt related variables should be significant prior to the introduction, and subsequent to the removal, of Capital Issues Controls. However, during the period when Governmental control over debt issues effectively substituted for contractual constraints, debt or leverage related variables are not expected to be important.

The 10 companies in the first sample represent a proportion of the listed public companies in Australia that may be said to have consolidated in the absence of any specific institutional requirements to do so (basically those N.S.W. and Victorian listed public companies for which information was available). This sample is investigated separately for a number of reasons. First, it is too small to allow any detailed statistical analysis. The most that can be hoped for is that with each company acting as its own control the hypothesized effects will be observable in "time" (i.e., as changes in the relevant variables). Second, so far as it is possible to ascertain these 10 companies were the first to consolidate. As such they are of interest in their own right. In this respect the smallness of the sample is an advantage since it becomes feasible to develop a detailed case study for each company. While the use of case studies as scientific evidence is fraught with difficulties (Campbell and Stanley, 1966, pp.6-7) they are employed here as a supplement to the analysis of changes referred to above.

The 44 N.S.W. companies that consolidated after 1941 likewise represent a proportion of the listed public companies in Australia that may be described as consolidating in the absence of any specific institutional requirements to do so. The difference between this and the above sample lies in the fact that while there was no legislative requirement to consolidate there was a Stock Exchange requirement to do so. These companies were however exempt from this requirement. This sample of consolidators is amenable to statistical analysis. This analysis takes place for both the period in which Capital Issues Controls were in place and that following, and for the pooled data. Chapter 2 also identifies a sample of 30 companies which could have consolidated but chose not to. This group of companies is employed as a control group against which the consolidators can be compared.

The principal problem with a cross-sectional comparison of this type is that it does not allow for random allocation to groups. In fact the members of both the sample and the control group self-select (i.e., either parent companies are consolidators or they are not). Characteristics related to this self selection (and omitted from explicit consideration) provide potential explanatory variables for any differences observed in the reporting behaviour of sample and control companies.[1] This issue is considered below. At this stage it need only be noted that the proposed cross-sectional comparisons are analogous to a Non-equivalent Control Group Design (Campbell and Stanley, 1966, p.47-50) which, while strictly a quasi-experimental design, rates relatively highly on most internal validity considerations.

---

1. Foster (1980, p.43) suggests that in these circumstances a firm profile analysis for both groups, in which the significance of financial and other differences between the groups is tested, be conducted. The problem with this "solution" is that the only stopping rule is an arbitrary one.

An additional problem is created by the fact that these cross-sectional comparisons are made in "event" time (i.e., time relative to the year in which a company first consolidates). The identification of this date for sample members is straightforward. The problem arises, however, as to what constitutes an appropriate comparison date for companies that decide not to consolidate. For non-consolidators that first acquired subsidiaries during the 1940-1962 period, the year of acquisition was defined to be the comparison date. For non-consolidators that possessed subsidiaries at the commencement of this period comparison dates were assigned randomly, but subject to the constraints that (a) the company possessed subsidiaries in the comparison year and (b) the time distribution of event dates for sample and control was approximately equal.

5.2 OMITTED VARIABLES

As observed above, correlated omitted variables constitute a threat to the internal validity of the tests of the hypotheses developed in Chapter 4. Chapter 7 considers in detail a number of alternative explanations for the consolidation phenomenon (overseas, auditor and taxation influences), and goes some way to alleviating the omitted variables problem. However, there are at least two other variables which, for reasons that will soon become obvious, have not been factored into the study.

5.2.1 Signalling Behaviour

Under essentially the same conditions as assumed in Chapter 4 (rational expectations, efficient capital markets) Ross (1977, 1979) considers managers' incentives to voluntarily disclose relevant information to outside markets. The argument proceeds as follows. If management possesses valuable information about the firm which is unavailable to the market it will have an incentive to release this information in order to increase the price of existing claims (issue price of any new claims) on the firm.[2] It will do so in such a manner that the market is able to discriminate between itself and similar firms with either no news or those that may be suppressing bad news. Indeed no news firms will have similar incentives i.e., to discriminate themselves from those with bad news. The managers of good news firms (the possessors of valuable information) will thus require a signal that (a) can be validated and (b) cannot be easily duplicated (i.e., one that is costly). The mechanism Ross relies on to achieve this result is the manager's personal guarantee - a guarantee effected through the operation of a compensation plan which ties managements' wealth to that of the firm. In group contexts such as those of interest here the adoption of a set of consolidated financial statements might serve much the same purpose.

The difficulty of relying on parent company financial statements as indicators of managerial performance or firm value in a group context has already been discussed. The moral hazard problem of falsely publishing good news is particularly pronounced. Bad news parents could, at relatively low cost,

2. That is, the firm faces a continuing problem of information asymmetry. The problem is not merely one of identifying the nature of new projects, but also one of identifying the current distribution of returns to the entire firm whenever additional financing is needed (refer Barnea, Haugen and Senbet, 1981, p.9).

manufacture profits through the appropriate choice of management fees, service charges, transfer prices etc. Consolidated financial statements provide a natural solution to this problem. First, not only is the production of a set of consolidated statements costly, it is also the case that a bad news group could not produce such statements without revealing that it was, in fact, a bad news group. Second, the signal could be validated through (at least) two mechanisms - (a) the external audit of group accounts or (b) following Ross (1977, 1979) by defining management compensation over group performance (see also section 4.2 _supra_).

Any difference between the actual price of a company's claims and the price that would prevail in an "informed" market is an agency cost associated with the informational asymmetry. As an agency cost of equity this information asymmetry only arises when there is separation of ownership from control. However this particular cost is not restricted to equity. It exists for the issue of any new claims on the firm including debt (though it was not directly considered in 4.1 or 4.2 _supra_).

Note that the information asymmetry arguments are directly related to the issue of debt or equity - as are the contracting explanations for consolidation developed in Chapter 4. Indeed, they are clearly not mutually exclusive hypotheses. This fact makes distinguishing between the two explanations very difficult. Unfortunately the implications of the information asymmetry arguments are not sufficiently well articulated to allow any assessment of their relative significance in the present context.[3]

5.2.2 Substitute Monitoring Mechanisms

Under the assumptions of Chapter 4 external suppliers of capital to the firm are indifferent to purchasing claims on the firm with, or without, monitoring facilities attached. This conclusion holds because in the world of perfect capital markets and rational expectations they postulate the external claim holders can "price protect". However, as Jensen and Meckling also observe (pp.323-325), even if external claimholders are indifferent it is unlikely that management will be since it can capture the benefits of writing and supplying monitoring contracts.

Among the principal monitoring arrangements available to management are:

(i) the publication of financial reports;

(ii) the appointment of external auditors;

(iii) the appointment of outside directors, and

(iv) the choice of stock exchange listing.[4]

This thesis is concerned with demand for the first. This demand will be affected by the extent to which these devices either substitute for, or complement, one another - and any analysis of this demand would normally be complicated by this fact. Fortunately, for the reasons discussed below, factors (ii)

---

3. Beaver (1981, Chapter 2) canvasses the complexity of the issues information asymmetry raises and the corresponding lack, as yet, of any clear empirical implications of this framework.

4. Refer to Watts (1977), Leftwich, Watts and Zimmerman (1981) and Chow (1982).

to (iv) may be regarded as common to all firms in the present study and therefore unlikely to constitute an ommitted variables problem.

Over the time period of this study all public companies were required to appoint an external auditor (and all of the companies in this study did so).[5] While companies had a choice of Stock Exchange upon which to list, the listing requirements were codified in 1925 and such differences as existed with respect to reporting obligations were marginal (refer Chapter 2.1.2). Finally, the appointment of outside directors in the sense in which this term is commonly employed (i.e., representatives of banks or insurance companies on the borrowing corporation's board) is not common practice in Australia. Since (ii) and (iv) are common to all firms in the present study, and (iii) is largely irrelevant, management's choice of financial reporting mechanism can be studied here without specifying the substitutability/ complementarity relations between alternative monitoring arrangements.

Of course, there are a number of ways in which the managers of a holding company may choose to report on the results of operations and present financial position. At one extreme they may choose simply to provide only the parent company's financial statements, with the investment in subsidiaries shown at cost. At

---

5. The Victorian Companies Act, 1896 included an auditing requirement; as did the NSW Companies Act, 1936. The Stock Exchanges required the appointment of an external auditor from 1912 (Official List Requirements (Sydney) - July 1912, 4(a)); although there was no specific mention of a separate audit report until 1929 (see also Aitken and Stokes (1984, pp.8-9)).

the other extreme they may choose to employ a full consolidation of the parent company and all of its subsidiaries. In between lie a number of alternatives including parent company and separate subsidiary accounts or a consolidation of less than 100 percent of subsidiaries with separate disclosure of the remaining subsidiaries' accounts.[6] The conditions under which managers would choose the full consolidation alternative are the principal concern of this study.

5.3 DATA COLLECTION

5.3.1 Case Studies: Pre-regulation Consolidators

A central theme of the thesis is that managements adopt the consolidated form of financial reporting because they are required to do so - explicitly or implicitly - by one or more of the financial contracts into which the firm has entered (i.e., consolidated financial statements are used to monitor performance under these contracts). Of major interest are the contracts written between:

(i) shareholders <u>inter se</u> (the Articles of Association),

(ii) shareholders and management (the management compensation scheme or service agreement), and

(iii) the shareholders (or management on their behalf) and their creditors (public or private).

These agreements may be referred to as part of a firm's "contract structure". The primary aim of the case studies is to determine

6. Historically the options have also included the aggregation (cf., consolidation) of parent and subsidiary accounts or the parent's accounts accompanied by an aggregation of the subsidiaries. These options were discussed in Chapter 2.1.2. and 2.3. Edwards and Webb (1984, p.55.) identify six alternative group reporting procedures adopted by U.K. companies between 1910-33.

whether or not there are any changes in this structure on or around the time of consolidation (i.e., whether or not any of these contracts exist in the sample firms and, if so, whether or not they have, or imply, a consolidation requirement).

The nature of the contracts being written is unlikely to be independent of the underlying structure of the firm and the environment in which it operates. Thus also of interest are changes in the nature of the firm itself on or around the time it elects to consolidate. Of particular concern in this regard are the evolution of the firm's:

(i) operating structure,
(ii) ownership structure, and
(iii) management structure.

The purpose of the case history is to describe - not to draw inferences or reach conclusions - this is left to the body of the study. For each firm the following search procedure is implemented:

Step 1: Access to individual company files at the relevant stock exchange (Sydney or Melbourne) is obtained. The company profile/history is initially developed from the information contained therein. The information available varies and may include any or all of the following:

(a) Listing Application and Shareholder Lists,
(b) Articles of Association,
(c) Service Agreement,
(d) Prospectuses,
(e) Annual Reports, and
(f) Investment Reviews.

Step 2: Gaps in the company profile are subsequently filled by reference to any or all of the following:

(a) Jobson's Year Book of Public Companies,
(b) Jobson's Investment Digest,
(c) The "Wildcat Monthly",
(d) Sydney Stock Exchange Official Gazette or the Official Record of the Stock Exchange of Melbourne,

(e) Archives at Melbourne University, Sydney University, Australian National University and the State Library of N.S.W. (Mitchell Library), and
(f) Company Archives and/or discussions with management.

The principal sources of the information contained in each case history are indicated at the completion of each. The case histories of the first 11 listed public companies to consolidate in the absence of any institutional requirements to do so (as indicated in Appendix I) appear in Appendix II in chronological order. Note that the absence of data on Ellis Caterers (South Australia) prohibits development of a profile for this firm.

5.3.2 Post-regulation Consolidators

Chapter 2.3 identifies 74 companies that reported the existence of subsidiaries at some time over the 1941-62 period. Of these 74 companies, 44 chose to consolidate for the first time during this period. For 15 of these companies the year of first consolidation coincided with the first acquisition of subsidiaries. Of the 30 companies choosing not to consolidate, 10 acquired their subsidiaries sometime between 1941 and 1962.

For consolidating companies data on each of the variables listed below was extracted for the year of, and that preceding, the decision to consolidate. For the 10 non-consolidators that acquired subsidiaries between 1941-62, data was likewise collected for the year of, and that preceding, the acquisition of the subsidiaries. For the remaining 20 non-consolidators arbitrary comparison dates were randomly assigned but so as to ensure that they were between 1941 and 1962 and that the company still had subsidiaries in the comparison year.

Tests of the hypotheses developed in Chapter 4 require data on each of the following variables:

H1: The presence or otherwise of cross-guarantees (CG).

H2: Management's percentage shareholding.

H3: (i) The existence or otherwise of a consolidation requirement in the company's Articles.

(ii) The existence or otherwise of a borrowing restriction in the company's Articles.

(iii) The existence and nature of any management compensation plans.

H4: The number, type and ownership of subsidiaries.

The extent to which data on each of these firm attributes was available varied considerably. For example the data required for H3 (i), (ii) and H(4) was generally available; that required for H3 (iii) was not. Consequently a direct test of this hypothesis was not possible. Tests of H1 and H2 required the use of proxy variables (as discussed subsequently).

In addition to the above data was also collected on the year in which subsidiaries were first acquired, the status of the parent company (operating or holding), the book value of investments in subsidiaries and inter-company advances, subsequent debt or equity issues, the year-end closing price of any listed securities, the financial statement effects of consolidation, assets-in-place, size (book and market values) and industry. The principal sources of this data were one or more of the companies annual accounts, the Sydney Stock Exchange Gazette, Jobson's Year Book of Public Companies and Jobson's Investment Digest, annual Stock Exchange company reviews, and the Stock Exchange files (including listing applications) for each company.

5.4 PROXY VARIABLES

As indicated above, tests of the two principal hypotheses (H1 and H2) require the use of proxy variables. For example, it was not always possible to establish unambiguously the existence of cross-guarantees in sample companies - as is required for a test of hypothesis 1. Fortunately, the analysis of Chapter 4.1 provides guidance as to what constitutes appropriate proxies. It was argued there that cross-guarantees were most likely to be found:

(a) between a parent and its wholly-owned subsidiaries,
(b) when the ratio of the proposed debt (X) to the assets-in-place (V_A) was relatively high.

It was usually possible to identify the number, type and extent of ownership (wholly-owned, less than wholly-owned) of a company's subsidiaries. Thus it was possible to calculate for each company the proportion of its subsidiaries that were wholly-owned (hereafter referred to as PRIVS). Similarly the ratio LEV = X/V_A, with:

X = book value of bank overdraft, mortgages, debentures and notes;
V_A = book value of land, buildings and equipment, net of depreciation.

was always determinable. Values for both PRIVS and LEV lie on a continuum between 0 and 1; as either or both variables increase, so does the probability that cross-guarantees will be present.

Tests of hypothesis 2 require identification of management's percentage shareholding in the firm, information not generally available. As is usual in studies of this type resort is made to a dichotomous classification of firms as being either "closely held/ owner controlled (0)" or "not closely held/manager controlled (1)".

Assignment of companies to categories occurred using the following rules. Firms were classified as owner controlled if one party owned 10 percent or more of the voting stock and exercised active control, or if one party owned 20 percent or more of the voting stock.[7] Active control was taken to mean representation on the Board of Directors or in the firm's management (i.e., managing director or company secretary). Of course, if a company's ordinary shares were not listed (9 instances) it was classified as owner-controlled. A firm was classified as "management-controlled" if it could not be identified as owner-controlled.

The classification of a company as owner-controlled assumes some importance. Since shareholder lists normally accompanied a listing application, at the time of listing this classification was relatively straightforward. However, as the time between initial listing and the decision to consolidate or not increased, it became more difficult to make this judgement - principally because shareholder lists for these later points in time were not generally available. Thus it became necessary to trace through time the composition of each company's Board of Directors and executive management (using most of the sources referred to in section 5.3.1) in an attempt to ascertain any "significant" changes in the distribution of decision-making power. Among the

7. A party was often a group of individuals with the same surname and often the same address. In such cases the party would usually hold a "large block" of the voting shares and a simple majority (including the managing directorship) on the Board of Directors. In fact the majority of the companies classified as "owner-controlled" were clearly "family-owned" companies, usually bearing the family name. The term "closely-held" is probably a more suitable description.

"family" controlled companies such changes were virtually non-existent. They were more common for the remaining companies and clearly considerable subjectivity is involved in the ultimate classification of these companies. To reduce the severity of problem the classification decision was made by two judges independently (the author and a graduate research assistant). In the 3 instances in which the judges disagreed the author's opinion prevailed. It was also possible to check the judgments for 10 of the cases with those made by Wheelwright (1957, 1966).[8] In each instance they agreed.

5.5 SUMMARY

The preceding discussion indicates that direct tests of hypotheses pertaining to management compensation plans are not feasible due to data availability constraints. Tests of hypotheses pertaining to information asymmetry, likewise, are not feasible - though the reason here is the absence of strong theory. However, tests of the remaining hypotheses are feasible and are described in the following Chapter.

---

8. Generally regarded as an Australian authority in this area, Wheelwright's decisions are based on the shareholder lists filed at the Registrar of Companies in each of these years.

CHAPTER 6

RESULTS

As indicated in the previous Chapter the empirical analysis takes place in a number of stages. Pre-disclosure regulation consolidators are considered first. The analysis of within group variation here is supplemented by detailed case studies. The larger sample of post-disclosure regulation consolidators/non-consolidators is considered next. The comparisons here take place within and between groups, both for the entire period and for sub-periods defined relative to Capital Issues Controls.

6.1 PRE-DISCLOSURE REGULATION SAMPLE

6.1.1 Univariate Analysis

Table 6.1 contains the results of the within group comparisons on the first 10 N.S.W. or Victorian companies to consolidate; all of which occurred prior to the introduction of Capital Issues Controls. The variables take the definitions assigned in Chapter 5.3 and 5.4.

Hypothesis 1 maintains that management would be more likely to consolidate in the presence of cross-guarantees. The detailed case studies contained in Appendix II indicate that in 4 cases consolidation followed the extension of cross-guarantees. In each instance leverage and the number of subsidiaries increased significantly. Cross-guarantees could also be identified in one other instance.

Given the arguments of Chapter 4.1, the likelihood of being joined as a guarantor will be determined largely by the borrowing company's leverage and whether its subsidiaries are wholly-owned

Table 6.1

Univariate Analysis : Pre-Regulation Sample (n = 10)

Variable	t_0	t_{-1}	Diff	One-tailed probabilities Wilcoxon	Paired-t
LEV	0.196 (0.197)	0.179 (0.219)	0.016 (0.149)	0.104	0.370
PRIVS	0.960 (0.105)	0.617 (0.483)	0.343 (0.472)	0.022	0.024
CTRL	0.400 (0.516)	0.100 (0.316)	0.300 (0.483)	0.054	0.040
SUBS	4.400 (4.088)	3.100 (3.872)	1.300 (1.829)	0.022	0.025

or not. Data on both proxies appears in Table 6.1. Consistent with hypotheses 1 and 4 both the number of subsidiaries (SUBS) and the proportion of these that were wholly-owned (PRIVS) were increasing in the year of consolidation; as was the amount of secured debt relative to the assets-in-place (LEV). The difference in means for the latter variable is heavily influenced by one instance of a company which actually retired debt (following an equity issue) in the year of consolidation. Leverage for this company fell from 0.49 to 0.11. For the remaining companies leverage either increased (6 cases) or remained steady (3 cases). The deletion of this case results in the leverage effect becoming significant. The difference in means increases to 0.060. This represents an average 34 percent increase in leverage. The associated Wilcoxon and Paired-t probabilities were 0.014 and 0.009 respectively.

Consistent with hypothesis 2 the CTRL variable indicates changes in ownership structure. In 3 cases firms changed from being owner to manager controlled. In a further 5 cases new equity issues occurred. Data relating to hypothesis 3 is discussed below. Briefly, in 4 of the 10 cases shareholder or shareholder-management contracts changed in a fashion that either implied or required consolidation.

6.1.2 Case Studies

Detailed case studies on the companies in Table 6.1 appear in Appendix II. The qualitative evidence contained therein suggests the following general conslusions. Consolidation followed closely (7/10 instances) a change in the underlying contracts into which the firm had entered. In many instances more than one such contract may have changed. For example, there were 3 instances of the creation of cross-guarantees, 1 in which the writing of a management compensation plan tied to "group" profits and cross-guarantees occurred concurrently, 2 in which Articles of Association were modified to require consolidation and 1 in which consolidation followed the writing of an agreement with preference shareholders relating to participation in "excess" profits. The Appendix also reveals that changes in the firm's underlying contractual structure were in the majority of cases preceded by either, or both, a change in the firm's operating (5/7) or ownership (5/7) structure. These observations support the arguments developed in Chapter 4 and are consistent the evidence presented in this Chapter.

6.2 POST-DISCLOSURE REGULATION SAMPLE

6.2.1 Profile Analysis

Chapter 2.3 identifies 74 companies that reported the

existence of subsidiaries some time between 1941-1962 and that did not reorganize and apply for relisting in Sydney, or subsequently apply for concurrent listing in Melbourne. Of these companies 44 decided to consolidate; 15 following the acquisition of their first subsidiaries and a further 5 following an increase in the number of subsidiaries. Ten of the 30 non-consolidators likewise acquired their first subsidiaries during this period.

Four of the consolidating companies were deleted from subsequent analysis. Two of these companies consolidated following the Taxation Commissioner's approval of a change in the balance dates of subsidiaries to align them with that of the parents. This was not a matter about which hypotheses had been developed in Chapter 4 and consequently their inclusion would have reduced the power of the tests of the contracting hypotheses. The remaining two companies consolidated following a change in their articles; including those relating to financial reporting. While these two cases are supportive of hypothesis 3 (i) they were the only two instances in which such a change was detected.[1] Their inclusion in tests of the remaining contracting hypotheses would simply add noise.

One of these instances warrants further consideration since it is particularly illustrative of the points made in Chapter 4.2 (i.e., equity related incentives to consolidate). Hadfields

---

1. The majority of changes in Articles that were detected during the data collection phase were updatings necessitated by reorganizations and relistings, or applications for additional listings (i.e., on the remaining Australian Exchanges). Thus as conjectured in Chapter 2.2 both the Sydney and Melbourne Stock Exchanges used these opportunities to induce changes in applicants' reporting behaviour.

(Australia) Ltd consolidated it's subsidiary, Australian Alloy Steel Ltd., following auditor queries regarding the appropriateness of:

(i) inter-company charges (totalling $60,000) reported in the separate accounts of the parent and its subsidiary;

(ii) the costing system used for allocating overheads between the two companies; and

(iii) the classification of certain expenditures (totalling $30,000) as "capital expenditures".

A sub-committee of the Board of Directors was commissioned to investigate the auditor's report. One of the matters this committee commented upon was the lack of disclosure regarding the subsidiary. The problems were ultimately attributed to "a peculiar and one sided agreement entered into by a past Board and the late Managing Director." There followed a reorganization and the adoption of a new set of articles - including upgraded reporting requirements.

Table 6.2 provides a frequency distribution of the "consolidation dates" for sample companies and a distribution of "assigned event dates" (refer Chapter 5.3.2) for the non-consolidators. Recall exact time period matching (i.e., by year) was not feasible and that non-consolidators have been assigned to years randomly subject to two constraints (a) the existence of subsidiaries and (b) the requirement that approximately equal proportions of companies fall into the pre/post 1951 periods.[2] With respect to the latter note that the proportions of consolidators (non-consolidators) falling into the pre/post 1951

2. Dropping criterion (b) and relying on strict random assignment (subject to (a)) does not change any of the substantive conclusions in this Chapter.

TABLE 6.2

Distribution of "Event" Dates 1941 - 1962

Year	Consolidators	Non-Consolidators
1941	-	-
1942	1	1
1943	-	2
1944	-	-
1945	1	1
1946	2	2
1947	2	-
1948	1	2
1949	2	1
1950	3	1
1951	1	1
1952	1	3
1953	-	1
1954	2	1
1955	2	2
1956	3	2
1957	6	3
1958	2	1
1959	4	2
1960	4	2
1961	2	1
1962	1	1
Totals	40	30

periods are 0.33(0.37)/0.67(0.63) respectively ($\chi^2 = 0.01$, $p > 0.90$).

The choice of the 1951 cut-off is dictated by the fact that institutional changes at this time imply non-stationarities in at least two of the independent variables. The decade of the 1940s was one of high tax rates and infrequent recourse to capital markets due to the Capital Issues Controls. In contrast by 1951 tax rates had been lowered, changes in the rates had become much less frequent and the Australian capital, and in particular the public debt, market had started to grow rapidly.[3] It was argued in Chapter 3 that the removal of Capital Issues Controls and the rapid development of the public debt market implied that leverage related variables were more likely to be significant in the post-, than in the pre -, 1951 period. The changes in the tax rates reinforce the choice of a 1951 cut-off. These changes are discussed in detail in Chapter 7.3.2 infra and Appendix III. Briefly it is observed in these sections that changes to the taxation system in the early 1950s created an incentive for companies to rely on multiple incorporation (i.e., create numerous subsidiaries). This suggests that SUBS is more likely to be a discriminating variable in the pre-, than in the post-, 1951 period.

Given the arguments of these sections it is not entirely surprising to observe that for both consolidators and non-

---

3. While Capital Issues Controls were not officially removed until December 1953 it is clear from Chapter 3 that they were not particularly restrictive in the very early 1950s. Indeed, many of the major developments in the market for public debt occurred as early as 1950-51.

consolidators the majority of pre-1951 companies set up their first subsidiaries during this period (9/13 and 7/11 respectively). The remaining companies had generally had subsidiaries for many years; and consistent with the arguments of Chapter 3 the majority chose to consolidate in a period in which there was both easier access to, and increased reliance on, external capital.

Table 6.3 provides summary statistics for the sample companies' balance sheet proportions and certain operating attributes. The scaling factor is firm value/size. The comparisons are based on parent company, not consolidated, figures since the latter do not exist for the non-consolidating group. The following definitions have been employed:

Value of Firm: the sum of the market value of the common and preferred stock (book value if not listed) and the book value of total current and long-term liabilities.

Total Debt: the book value of total current and long-term liabilities.

Secured Debt: the book value of bank overdraft, mortgages, debentures and notes.

Fixed Assets: the book value of land, buildings, plant and equipment - net of depreciation.

Investments in Subsidiaries: the book value of the net investment in subsidiaries (i.e., shares plus (minus) loans to (from) subsidiaries).

Table 6.3 indicates that there is little to differentiate consolidators from non-consolidators in terms of their capital structures. There were no significant differences in the

TABLE 6.3

Profile Analysis of Sample Firms

Variable	Group Mean (Std Devn)		Two-tailed Probabilities	
	Consolidators	Non-Consolidators	Mann-Whitney	Student's t
Total Debt/ Firm Value	0.285 (0.177)	0.300 (0.177)	0.794	0.721
Secured Debt/ Firm Value	0.123 (0.129)	0.102 (0.120)	0.490	0.489
Fixed Assets/ Firm Value	0.282 (0.265)	0.420 (0.305)	0.035	0.047
Investment in Subsidiaries/ Firm Value	0.237 (0.309)	0.138 (0.204)	0.107	0.135
Total Subsidiaries	3.025 (4.660)	1.633 (1.520)	0.016	0.121
n	40	30		

proportion of total or secured debt between the groups.[4] In contrast, consolidating parents have a significantly lower proportion of net fixed assets (assets-in-place) than non-consolidating parents; and there is some evidence that they have a higher proportion of their funds tied up in subsidiaries[5] (i.e., in assets "not-in-place"). It was argued in Chapter 4 that capital or asset structures <u>per se</u> are not important; rather it is the relationship between them and, in particular, between the amount of secured debt and the assets available for satisfaction

4. The argument in the text does not lead to strong priors on these variables, hence the reporting of two-tailed probabilities. Pooled variance estimates are used throughout.

5. Together Tables 6.3 and 6.5 indicate that on a consolidated basis there is no significant difference in the proportion of net fixed assets in both groups - consolidators 0.442, non-consolidators 0.420.

of that debt (assets-in-place or net fixed assets) that is important. Differences along this dimension are subsequently reported.

Table 6.3 also reveals that consolidators have more subsidiaries than non-consolidators. Note that the mean number of subsidiaries for the consolidating group is affected by one company with 27 subsidiaries. Deleting this outlier or effecting a square root transformation leaves this difference significant.[6]

Table 6.4 provides information on the size distribution of sample companies in both book and market value terms. It is apparent that these distributions are highly skewed (for both groups and both measures). While the quartile distribution suggests consolidators may be larger than non-consolidators, the significance tests indicate otherwise. A logarithmic transformation of the size variables also suggests no significant difference.[7]

---

6. The results of these procedures may be summarized as follows (two-tailed probabilities):

	Consolidators	Non-Consolidators	Mann-Whitney	Student's t
Deletion of Outlier	2.410 (2.603)	1.633 (1.520)	0.044	0.148
Square root transformation	1.516 (0.863)	1.199 (0.450)	0.016	0.071

7. The results of this transformation were as follows (two-tailed probabilities):

	Consolidators	Non-Consolidators	Mann-Whitney	Student's t
log($Mkt Value)	5.957 (0.607)	5.848 (0.582)	0.373	0.453
log($Bk Value)	5.930 (0.515)	5.827 (0.540)	0.349	0.421

TABLE 6.4

Size Distributions - Book and Market Value Quartiles

Market Value ($x10^4$)	Mean (Std Devn)	Min	25th	50th	75th	Max
Consolidators	210.4 (314.1)	28.7	36.5	82.8	230.1	1382.0
Non Consolidators[A]	179.2 (366.6)	5.1	28.9	64.8	163.1	1985.0
Book Value ($x10^4$)						
Consolidators	154.4 (208.1)	4.5	34.2	104.1	198.8	1260.0
Non-Consolidators[B]	153.8 (329.8)	4.5	31.6	68.2	139.0	1841.5

A. Mann-Whitney and Student's probabilities (two-tailed) of 0.373 and 0.704 respectively.
B. Mann-Whitney and Student's probabilities (two-tailed) of 0.993 and 0.349 respectively.

Table 6.5 illustrates the financial statement effects of consolidation. Note that firm value is estimated using both the market and book values of equity. On average, consolidation was both asset and income increasing.[8] It also had the effect of increasing the amount of both secured and total debt in a firm's capital structure - by bringing in that of the subsidiaries. The ratio of secured debt to assets-in-place also increases, though not significantly so.

At this point it is convenient to note that there is little support for alternative hypothesis 1 in the data. First, while consolidation is income increasing, income based restrictive covenants are relatively uncommon in Australian debt contracts

8. The same result obtains for log transformations on these variables.

TABLE 6.5

Financial Statement Effects of Consolidation (t_o)

Variables	Group Mean (Std Dev'n)		One-tailed Probabilities	
	Parent	Consolidated	Wilcoxon	Student's t
Firm Value(Mkt)	2,103,690 (3,141,123)	2,241,835 (3,210,973)	0.000	0.013
Firm Value(Bk)	1,543,624 (2,081,481)	1,886,490 (2,354,842)	0.000	0.002
Net Profit*	81,464 (94,458)	105,353 (166,774)	0.000	0.061
EPS_{to}*	0.123 (0.100)	0.141 (0.095)	0.000	0.049
Total Debt/$_{FV(Mkt)}$	0.285 (0.177)	0.352 (0.156)	0.000	0.013
Secured Debt/$_{FV(Mkt)}$	0.123 (0.129)	0.150 (0.136)	0.002	0.017
Fixed Assets/$_{FV(Mkt)}$	0.448 (0.265)	0.442 (0.268)	0.000	0.000
Secured Debt/$_{N.F.A.}$	0.293 (0.291)	0.328 (0.253)	0.058	0.134
n	40			

*Net Profit has pairwise deletion on 2 missing consolidated figures (i.e., n = 38).

(Whittred and Zimmer, 1985). Second, rather than being leverage reducing (as predicted by an hypothesis based on opportunism) consolidation is, on average, leverage increasing. Across the sample leverage fell in only 11 instances (28 percent of cases).[9] Further, while in 6 of these instances reported leverage was over the (relatively standard) 40 percent limit, in only one of these cases was leverage brought below this limit by consolidation. Strictly speaking, these observations do not allow rejection of an hypothesis based on opportunism. As observed in Chapter 4.4 the issue is one of relative significance; and there is little to suggest that ex post opportunism is a significant determinant of the consolidation decision in this data.

TABLE 6.6

Industry Representation

Industry	Consolidators	Non-Consolidators
Financier	5	2
General Engineering	2	4
Printing and Allied Industries	2	3
Bakers, Flour Millers	1	2
General Retailers	7	5
Motor Accessories	2	1
Timber Merchants, Sawmillers	2	-
Pure Holding Company	9	3
Other	10	10
Totals	40	30

9. Leverage increased 17 times and remained steady 12 times. The latter cases were evenly spread over those which had no secured debt and those in which all secured borrowing was undertaken by the parent company.

Table 6.6 provides the industry representation of both groups. Any industry in which there was more than one company is separately disclosed. With one exception (Timber Merchants, Sawmillers) every such industry was represented in both samples. Further, apart from the higher (though not significantly so) proportion of pure holding companies in the consolidating group (χ^2 = 1.886, p = 0.170) there does not appear to be an industry effect in the data - just as there is no size effect. Thus to the extent that any omitted variables (e.g., political costs) may be related to either of these two factors they are unlikely to represent a major problem in subsequent analysis.

6.2.2 Univariate Tests - Pooled Data

Table 6.8 contains the results of the univariate analysis on the post-regulation sample. However before turning to this analysis it is worth noting some of the distributional properties

TABLE 6.7

Descriptive Statistics on Variables Used in Univariate Analysis : Consolidators (40), Non-Consolidators (30)

	LEV		PRIVS		CTRL		SUBS	
	Cons	Non-Cons	Cons	Non-Cons	Cons	Non-Cons	Cons	Non-Cons
Mean	0.293	0.181	0.962	0.695	0.700	0.267	3.025	1.633
Median	0.254	0.147	1.000	0.750	1.000	0.000	2.000	1.000
Std.Dev'n	0.291	0.213	0.163	0.424	0.464	0.450	4.660	1.520
Min.	0.000	0.000	0.000	0.000	0.000	0.000	1.000	1.000
Max.	0.971	0.859	1.000	1.000	1.000	1.000	27.000	7.000

of the independent variables. Table 6.7 provides relevant statistics.

While the differences in the means are in the predicted direction and are reflected in the corresponding medians, the data indicate considerable skewness in each of the independent variables. Since all of the statistical tests employed subsequently rely on an assumption of symmetry (if not normality) some caution is required in interpreting the results.[10]

Turning now to Table 6.8 note that between group comparisons (and the associated Mann-Whitney and Student's t statistics) are obtained by reading down columns. Within group comparisons (and the associated Wilcoxon and Paired - t statistics) are obtained by reading across rows. All probabilities are one-tailed.

Hypothesis 1 pertains to cross-guarantees. Fourteen consolidators (3 non-consolidators) could be identified as having cross-guarantees. Adopting the extremely conservative assumption that if the presence of cross-guarantees could not be established then there were none, a Chi-square test reveals this difference to be significant (X^2=4.547, $p < 0.05$). At the other extreme, if it is assumed that in addition to the above all overdrafts are accompanied by cross-guarantees (a relatively common bank practice) then the relative frequencies in the groups become 33/40 and 17/30 respectively. Once again, this difference is significant (X^2=4.412, $p < 0.05$).

---

10. The options for normalizing transformations are also severely limited given the 0/1 limits (natural or imposed) on three of the four variables.

TABLE 6.8

Univariate Analysis - Main Effects

Group	Mean (Std Dev'n) t_0	t_{-1}	Diff	One-tailed probabilities Wilcoxon	Paired-t
	Panel A : LEV				
Consolidators	0.293 (0.291)	0.225 (0.278)	0.068 (0.206)	0.022	0.022
Non-consolidators	0.181 (0.213)	0.173 (0.209)	0.008 (0.095)	0.294	0.334
Mann-Whitney	0.067	0.368	0.139		
Student's t	0.039	0.197	0.071		
	Panel B : PRIVS				
Consolidators	0.962 (0.163)	0.607 (0.481)	0.355 (0.485)	0.001	0.000
Non-consolidators	0.695 (0.424)	0.395 (0.455)	0.300 (0.466)	0.004	0.001
Mann-Whitney	0.001	0.032	0.335		
Student's t	0.000	0.033	0.317		
	Panel C : CTRL				
Consolidators	0.700 (0.464)	n.a.	n.a.	n.a.	n.a.
Non-consolidators	0.267 (0.450)	n.a.	n.a.	n.a.	n.a.
Mann-Whitney	0.000	n.a.	n.a.		
Student's t	0.000	n.a.	n.a.		
	Panel D : SUBS				
Consolidators	3.025 (4.660)	2.125 (3.517)	0.900 (1.751)	0.000	0.000
Non-consolidators	1.633 (1.520)	1.300 (1.685)	0.333 (0.547)	0.003	0.000
Mann-Whitney	0.008	0.307	0.058		
Student's t	0.061	0.120	0.045		

The results on the cross-guarantee proxies appear in Panels A and B of Table 6.8. It is apparent that consolidators tend to be over 50 percent more highly geared than non-consolidators in the year of consolidation. This difference does not exist in the preceding year. In the year of consolidation the subsidiaries of the consolidators also tend to be wholly-owned. In fact only 4 consolidators had subsidiaries which were not wholly-owned. The corresponding figure for the non-consolidators was 12. A χ^2 statistic reveals this difference to be significant (χ^2=8.875, p = 0.003). The difference also exists in both years.

Hypothesis 1 also refers to a consolidation of the borrowing company and its guarantors - which may or may not be the same thing as a consolidation of the company and its subsidiaries. They would coincide if all subsidiaries were guarantors which, given the arguments of Chapter 4.1, is likely to be the case here since the subsidiaries of the consolidators were essentially wholly-owned.

Additional information on the sample firm's capital structures appears in Table 6.9 which contains frequency distributions of sources of long-term debt finance. Companies were classified into those that relied on overdraft finance only, a single source of debt other than overdraft, multiple sources and those that had no long-term debt in their capital structure. With the latter exception, all the debt was secured in one form or another e.g., legal/equitable mortgage or cross-guarantees (with or without a supporting equitable mortgage). Note also that in the majority of cases the debt appeared in the parent company's books (i.e., the parent was usually the financier for the group).

However, those few instances in which the debt appeared in the subsidiaries are also included in the Table. Thus a group in which a subsidiary relied on an overdraft, and the parent raised debenture capital, would be classified as relying on multiple sources of finance.

TABLE 6.9

Frequency Distributions: Sources of Finance

Source	Consolidators	(Non Consolidators)
Overdraft only	15	(13)
Non-overdraft only	3	(4)
Multiple	18	(3)
None	4	(10)
Totals	40	(30)

Table 6.9 reveals significant differences in the pattern of financing between the groups (X^2 = 12.396, p = 0.006). The first that becomes apparent is that consolidators are much more likely to have some form of secured debt in their capital structure than non-consolidators - 36 (90%), compared to 20 (67%) companies respectively. A Chi-square test on this dimension provides X^2 = 5.833, p = 0.016. Similarly, consolidators are much more likely to have relied upon multiple sources of long-term debt - 18 (45%) compared to 3 (10%) respectively (X^2 = 10.000, p = 0.002). Consolidating companies classified in this category typically

relied on a bank overdraft and either a mortgage loan provided by a bank or insurance company (11); or some form of public debt (i.e., debentures or notes (7)). A further 2 of the consolidators relied on public debt - meaning 9 of the 36 consolidators that borrowed relied on an offer to the public. In contrast, none of the 20 non-consolidators that borrowed did so in this fashion. A Chi-square test reveals this difference to be significant ($X^2 = 5.96$, $p = 0.012$).

Hypothesis 2 maintains that closely-held (owner-controlled) corporations would be less likely to consolidate than widely-held (manager-controlled) corporations. Using a 0/1 dummy variable (CTRL) and the definitions given in Chapter 5.4, it is clear that there are significant differences between the groups on this dimension in the predicted direction. Only 12 consolidators were identified as being owner-controlled. In contrast, 22 non-consolidators were so classified. A Chi-square test reveals these proportions to be significantly different ($X^2 = 14.452$, $p = 0.000$).[11] So far as it was possible to ascertain there was no change in the control status of parent companies in the year they elected to consolidate (i.e., this factor exhibited no within group variation).

Hypothesis 3 holds that consolidation was more likely if a company's Articles included either a consolidation requirement or certain kinds of borrowing restrictions; or if there was a

---

11. Any measurement error in this variable is most likely attributable to the classification of companies as "manager-controlled". The "owner-controlled" companies were usually readily identifiable as such - not only from such shareholder lists as were available but also from the independent sources reviewed for each company (as described in Chapter 5.4).

compensation scheme which remunerated management on the basis of group performance. Data on compensation plans was not available and, as indicated earlier, this hypothesis was not tested. A survey of the Articles of Association that were available (30/40 consolidators) revealed:

(a) that in no instance was there a borrowing restriction of a kind (as described in Chapter 4.2) likely to induce a consolidation;[12] and

(b) apart from the two instances previously referred to (Section 6.2.1) there were no instances in which an explicit modification of reporting requirements preceded consolidation.

Resting on an assumption that monitoring costs increase more rapidly than the costs of consolidation, hypothesis 4 maintains that the likelihood of consolidation is increasing in the number of subsidiaries. The profile analysis has already indicated significant differences between the groups in the number (and degree of ownership) of subsidiaries. Table 6.8 indicates that this difference does not appear to exist in the year preceding consolidation. The number of subsidiaries per company was increasing in both groups in the year of consolidation. However, it was increasing at almost twice the rate for consolidators as it was for non-consolidators.[13] Further, the vast majority of the

---

12. This provides support for Collin's (1940) observation that in the majority of cases companies adopted their own Articles and excluded the operation of Table A of the Companies Act (refer Chapter 4.2 <u>supra</u>).

13. Similar results are obtained using the square root transformation.

newly created subsidiaries for the consolidating group were wholly-owned, in contrast to those of the non-consolidators. Both of these observations are consistent with the hypothesized effects of these variables.

6.2.3 Univariate Tests - By Sub-period

The analysis in Table 6.8 is based on data pooled from a 22 year period and involves strong stationarity assumptions on each of the major variables of interest. It has already been observed that there are reasons for believing both LEV and SUBS to be time-dependent - with time defined relative to 1951. Table 6.10 breaks down the pooled results into those for the pre- and post- 1951 periods.

The results in Table 6.10 suggest that stationarity is a reasonable assumption for only the CTRL variable. The non-stationarities in LEV and SUBS are consistent with expectations formed on the basis of the institutional changes occurring around

Table 6.10

Sub-period Analysis of Main Effects
Mean (std Dev'n)

	1941 - 1951		1952 - 1962	
	Consolidators	Non-Consolidators	Consolidators	Non-Consolidators
LEV	0.210 (0.292)	0.233 (0.266)	0.333 (0.288)	0.151 (0.177)*
PRIVS	0.961 (0.075)	0.818 (0.405)	0.963 (0.193)	0.623 (0.429)*
CTRL	0.769 (0.439)	0.273 (0.467)*	0.667 (0.480)	0.263 (0.452)*
SUBS	4.846 (7.244)	1.000 (0.000)*	2.148 (2.429)	2.000 (1.826)
n	13	11	27	19

* Between group comparison significant at $\alpha = 0.05$ using one-tailed Mann-Whitney and Student's-t tests.

1951. That is, during the period Capital Issues Controls were in place (1941-1951) LEV was not a significant explanatory variable. Yet it was both before the introduction, and after the removal, of these controls. Likewise the taxation incentives for multiple incorporation in the post- 1951 period eliminate the power of SUBS as an explanatory variable. There is no obvious explanation for the behaviour of PRIVS.

6.3 MULTIVARIATE TESTS

As a check on the univariate results reported above the impact of each of the variables was also assessed by including them in the pooled cross-sectional probit regressions indicated in Table 6.11. Sub-period regressions were not performed because of the small sample sizes. The dependent variable in these regressions was a 0-1 dummy variable representing consolidation status (0 = non-consolidator, 1 = consolidator). The application of probit to the study of accounting policy choices is discussed in detail in Hagerman and Zmijewski (1979) and Bowen, Noreen and Lacey (1981). As observed in these studies the procedure overcomes the problems (heteroskedasticity) associated with OLS regression using a dichotomous dependent variable by transforming it in such a way that it has an underlying continuous distribution. Maximum Likelihood Estimators can then be obtained which are consistent, asymptotically efficient and have a known sampling distribution. Whether or not the same benefits obtain with highly skewed independent variables is a moot point since little is known of the sensitivity of probit to violations of its underlying assumptions. The results of these regressions must be

TABLE 6.11

Multivariate Analysis
Probit Parameter Estimates
(Asymptotic t - statistics)

Variable (Predicted Sign)	Intercept (?)	LEV (+)	PRIVS (+)	CTRL (+)	SUBS (+)	RTSUBS (+)	χ^2 (d.f.)	R^2 (Correctly Classified)
Model 1	-2.828	1.311	2.092	1.044	0.185		28.82*	0.337
	(-2.992)$^{+}$	(1.657)$^{+++}$	(2.564)$^{+}$	(2.927)$^{+}$	(1.350)$^{+++}$		(4)	(74.3%)
Model 2	-3.489	1.367	2.146	1.038		0.745	29.54*	0.345
	(-2.956)$^{+}$	(1.710)$^{++}$	(2.597)$^{+}$	(2.894)$^{+}$		(1.601)$^{+++}$	(4)	(74.3%)

* Exceeds 99th percentile of χ^2 distribution.
\+ Significant at $\alpha = 0.01$ (one-tailed)
++ Significant at $\alpha = 0.05$ (one-tailed)
+++ Significant at $\alpha = 0.10$ (one-tailed)

interpreted with this in mind.

All of the signs are in the predicted direction and the variables are significant at conventional levels. The proxies for the presence of cross-guarantees receive the highest weightings (as predicted) followed by CTRL and SUBS. The square root transformation on the latter variable has little effect on the overall regressions, though it increases the level of significance of SUBS.[14]

Table 6.12 contains univariate correlation coefficients for the independent variables used in the regressions. Given the skewness observed earlier most weight is placed on the Spearman Rank correlation coefficients. With the exception of SUBS and RTSUBS which, not surprisingly, exhibit very high correlation (perfect in rank order); the independent variables are essentially uncorrelated. Overall, the models are highly significant and possess a reasonable amount of explanatory power ($R^2 > 0.33$). As in earlier studies Table 6.11 also reports the percentage of firms correctly classified by the models. In the absence of a hold-out sample it is important to recognise that this statistic is overstated since it is estimated using the sample from which the models were developed. Bearing this in mind it is still the case that the multivariate models perform well - in the sense that they significantly outperform univariate models based on any of the independent variables.

---

14. The corresponding ordinary least squares regressions were also performed, with essentially the same results. For example, the 4 variable regression which incorporated LEV, PRIVS, CTRL and SUBS had relative weights (t-statistics) of 0.266 (1.367), 0.476 (3.009), 0.332 (3.206) and 0.109 (1.540) respectively. The R^2 for this regression was 0.336.

TABLE 6.12

Correlation Matrices: Pearson and Spearman (Two-tailed Probability)

PANEL A : Pearson Correlation

	LEV	PRIVS	CTRL	SUBS	RTSUBS
LEV	1				
PRIVS	0.076 (0.533)	1			
CTRL	0.041 (0.734)	0.239 (0.047)	1		
SUBS	0.231 (0.054)	0.023 (0.853)	0.020 (0.870)	1	
RTSUBS	0.202 (0.093)	0.003 (0.981)	0.083 (0.494)	0.962 (0.001)	1

PANEL B : Spearman Correlation

	LEV	PRIVS	CTRL	SUBS	RTSUBS
LEV	1				
PRIVS	0.121 (0.320)	1			
CTRL	0.007 (0.954)	0.181 (0.134)	1		
SUBS	0.033 (0.789)	-0.214 (0.076)	0.174 (0.149)	1	
RTSUBS	0.033 (0.789)	-0.214 (0.076)	0.174 (0.149)	1.000 (0.000)	1

The absence of time-series variation in the variable CTRL means that "change in reporting behaviour" can only be regressed on "change in LEV, PRIVS and SUBS". The results of these regressions (not reported) indicate that both "change in LEV" and "change in SUBS (or RTSUBS)" are significant; though at lower levels than in the univariate analysis above. The overall regressions are still significant, though the R^2's drop to as little as 6-8 percent.[15]

6.4 SUMMARY

The preceding results indicate support for the three principal hypotheses of Chapter 4. The likelihood of consolidation is significantly and positively related to the presence of cross-guarantees; and significantly and inversely related to management's proportionate shareholding. The likelihood of consolidation is also increasing in the number (and type) of subsidiaries. However, the relative significance of these factors has changed over time. Consolidators during the 1940s were characterized by the separation of ownership from control and a larger number of subsidiaries. The latter difference disappeared following the introduction of taxation incentives for multiple incorporation in the early 1950s. With the concurrent freeing up of the market for public debt consolidators could be characterized by both "separation" and an increasing reliance on debt that was "publicly placed".

---

15. The corresponding least squares regressions yield the same result.

CHAPTER 7

ALTERNATIVE HYPOTHESES

It was argued in Chapter 3 that the content of a firm's debt contracts and the nature of its ownership structure are important determinants of management's choice of reporting method. However, there are other factors that might also affect this choice e.g., disclosure regulations or other institutional influences such as the practices of particular audit firms, overseas influences and taxation. The sample selection criteria employed in Chapter 2 rule out regulation as an explanatory variable. The arguments surrounding each of the remaining factors are developed and evaluated empirically below.

7.1 OVERSEAS INFLUENCES

One reason that an Australian holding company might consolidate its results is that such a consolidation is required for the purposes of an overseas parent who has already adopted this form of financial reporting. Note the implicit assumptions here. First, it is assumed that the overseas parent is already consolidating. Second, it is assumed that the results of foreign subsidiaries are to be included in this consolidation. Third, it is assumed that the Australian parent can perform its consolidation at lower cost than the overseas parent.

It has already been observed (Chapter 2.1.1) that the financial reporting practices of public companies in the U.S. and U.K. preceded those of Australian companies by some decades. To the extent that the parents of Australian holding companies were of either origin, assumption 1 seems likely to hold. Likewise, assumption 3 seems quite plausible. However assumption 2 is problematic since in both the U.S. and the U.K. such standards on consolidation as exist have always permitted the exclusion of subsidiaries from the consolidation on a number of grounds - including exchange restrictions or otherwise impaired control of assets; if their inclusion would be misleading; materiality and impracticality (including disproportionate expense or delay).[1]

Despite these observations this matter is, in principle, resolvable by appeal to the evidence. If overseas influences of this type are important it seems reasonable to hypothesize that:

H5: Australian holding companies which chose to consolidate were more likely to have an overseas parent than those holding companies which chose not to consolidate.

It was not possible to obtain direct evidence on the extent of overseas holdings in Australian companies. Even if shareholder lists were available there could be no guarantee that it would be possible to accurately identify such interests (due to nominee holdings, etc.). Thus the strategy employed involved reading every "Investment Review" contained in a company's Stock Exchange file for the period of interest and, of course, the Jobson's Year Book entries. This search was unable to identify any reference to the presence of overseas holdings in any of the 70 companies involved.[2] On the other hand it did establish that 7 of the consolidators (3 of the non-consolidators) acquired overseas

---

1. Refer, for example, to Accounting Research Bulletin No.51, Consolidated Financial Statements in the U.S. and Statement of Standard Accounting Practice No.14 Group Accounts (and its predecessors) in the U.K.

2. In contrast, there is some evidence of overseas influences in the pre-regulation sample (see Appendix II).

subsidiaries at some stage during the period. Such arrangements could be an indirect source of overseas influence (e.g., if the subsidiary had to comply with listing or reporting requirements in the foreign State). However, a χ^2 test reveals there to be no significant difference in the proportion of such subsidiaries in the two groups ($\chi^2 = 0.788$, $p = 0.375$).

7.2 AUDIT FIRM EFFECTS[3]

There are at least two ways in which audit firms might have an effect on the decision to consolidate. The first argument (referred to subsequently as the auditor - advocate hypothesis) maintains that the reason firms consolidate is that their auditors "compel" them to do so (i.e., the auditors adopt a position on what constitutes adequate financial reporting and they are ultimately able to convince management/directors to adopt this form of reporting).[4] Note that this hypothesis implies an association between consolidation/non-consolidation and auditors (audit firms) that can be identified as consolidation-advocates/non-consolidation advocates respectively. Note that this naive hypothesis also implies no cross-sectional or time-series variation in an auditor's preferred position. A more

3. General references for this section include Graham (1978), Goldberg (1981) and Gibson (1967).

4. Both analytically and empirically this position is difficult to sustain. First, the responsibility for the accounts is ultimately the Directors' not the auditor's. Second, the question arises as to not only how the auditors could compel Directors to do something they are not required by law to do, but why they would want to do so. At an empirical level there is no direct evidence in any of the companies studied in this study of either auditor pressure to consolidate or of an auditor qualifying his/her report for non-consolidation.

sophisticated hypothesis would allow auditors to exercise their judgement about the appropriate form of financial reporting conditional upon the attendant circumstances. In this case the auditor could well be influencing management's decision but there would not necessarily be an association between audit firm and the consolidation/non-consolidation decision <u>per se</u> (i.e., the auditor/audit firm, depending on portfolio mix, could be represented in both samples of companies).[5]

Unfortunately this more sophisticated form of the auditor-effect hypothesis is not testable. In contrast, provided auditor advocates/non-advocates can be identified the auditor-advocate hypothesis is. Thus:

> H6: Australian holding companies which chose to consolidate were more likely to have an auditor who advocated consolidation than those holding companies which chose not to consolidate.

Note that the rejection of this particular hypothesis does not constitute a rejection of an audit firm effect.

As discussed above a test of this hypothesis requires the identification of auditor-advocates. This task has already been (partly) performed by Gibson (1967, Chapter 21). In his discussion of the evolution of holding companies' reporting practices Gibson (1971, pp.279-80) documents the divided views of the accounting profession on the 1938 Victorian Act. The Victorian State Council of the Institute of Chartered Accountants made it known it was opposed to the presentation of consolidated financial statements. The Commonwealth Institute of Accountants on the other hand supported this proposal. Additionally a number

5. As is the case in the samples studied here.

of prominent accountants made their positions known - either on the reporting requirements of the proposed Victorian Act per se or on the annual reports of some of the earliest companies to consolidate.[6] Gibson identifies (pp.276-279) A.H. Outhwaite, J.V.M. Wood and W.H. Jolly as prominent accountants opposed to consolidated financial reporting. However, during the same period contributions to the professional journals (The Commonwealth Journal of Accountancy and The Chartered Accountant in Australia) by A.A. Fitzgerald (1936), G.E. Fitzgerald (1938) and D.M. Ferguson (1931) all favoured consolidation. An even earlier contribution by E.V. Nixon (1928) had favoured the alternative of a legal balance sheet, supplemented by an aggregate statement of the assets and liabilities of the subsidiaries.

Not surprisingly the contributions to the professional literature following the 1938 Act concentrated principally on the procedural aspects of consolidation. Chief among these were three series of articles - the first by G.E. Fitzgerald and A.E. Speck (1944, 1945),[7] the second by R.K. Yorston (1947) and the third by G.E. Fitzgerald (1950, 1951). A.A. Fitzgerald maintained his contribution to this literature and articles on the topic by R.A. Irish (1943) and Spence (1949, 1958) also appeared.

The professional and academic affiliations of the principal contributors to the consolidation debate (as identified in Gibson

---

6. For example, through press coverage of the type cited by Gibson (1971, p.276) of the annual general meeting at which Dunlop Perdriau presented its first consolidated accounts.

7. See also Gibson (1967, p.306). This series of articles formed the basis of what was, for several decades, the leading textbook on the subject in Australia.

TABLE 7.1

Professional and Academic Affiliations of Principal Contributors to the Consolidation Debate, 1928-1960

Contributors (Alphabetically)	Professional Status	Audit Firm	Head Office
Ferguson, D.M.	F.C.A.	E.V. Nixon and Partners	Melbourne
Fitzgerald, A.A. (Sir)[1]	F.C.A.	Fitzgerald and Thompson	Melbourne
Fitzgerald, G.E.[1]	F.C.A.	Fitzgerald and Thompson	Melbourne
Irish, R.A. (Sir)	F.C.A.	R.A. Irish and Michelmore	Sydney
*Jolly, W.A.	F.C.A.	Robinson and Jolly	Brisbane
Nixon, E.V. (Sir)[1]	F.C.A.	E.V. Nixon and Partners	Melbourne
*Outhwaite, A.H.[1]	F.C.A.	Young and Outhwaite	Melbourne
Speck, A.E.[1,2]	F.A.S.A.	n.a.	Melbourne
Spence, J.D.	A.C.A.	E.V. Nixon and Partners	Melbourne
*Wood, J.V.M.	F.C.A.	J.V.M. Wood and Co.	Melbourne
Yorston, R.K. (Sir)[1,3]	F.C.A.	Sole Practitioner	Sydney

Source: Institute of Chartered Accountants in Australia, Register of Members (various editions).

Legend:
* = Opposed Consolidation
F.C.A. = Fellow, Institute of Chartered Accountants in Australia
A.C.A. = Associate, Institute of Chartered Accountants in Australia
F.A.S.A. = Fellow, Australian Society of Accountants

Footnotes:
1. University of Melbourne Commerce Graduate and/or Lecturer in Accounting, University of Melbourne.
2. Tutorial Manager, Hemmingway Robertson Institute.
3. Principal, Australian Accountancy College.

(1967) and from a survey of the professional literature) are provided in Table 7.1. With the exception of Speck all the contributors were members of the Institute. With the further exception of Spence all the contributors were principals in public practice.[8] Table 7.1 serves to identify the consolidation advocates (and for the pre-1938 period the non-consolidation advocates) and provides the basis for ascertaining whether an auditor-advocate effect exists in the companies identified in Chapter 2.[9]

Not one of the auditors identified in Table 7.1 appears in either group of companies in the year of, or that preceding, the decision to consolidate. Table 7.2 presents the frequency distributions of audit firms in the samples. It is clear that a large number of separate audit firms were involved - 31 in the case of the consolidators, 27 in the case of the non-consolidators. There was, however, a group of 9 audit firms that conducted approximately 50 percent of the audits in <u>both</u> samples. These firms (the firms with multiple audits) are identified in

---

8. Spence at the time of his contributions was an academic, but gave his mailing address on the Institute's Register as c/- E.V. Nixon and Partners.

9. Whether or not an auditor-advocate effect exists it is apparent from Table 7.1 that a "Melbourne effect" exists within auditing firms. This is unlikely to be independent of the fact that they were the first to confront the practical problems of consolidation. However the effect manifests itself in another fashion also. Among the 8 advocates of consolidation no less than 5 were either graduates of, or Lecturers in Accounting at, the University of Melbourne - arguably the leading "Accounting Department" in the country during this period. Goldberg (1981) comments in some detail on the Melbourne influence. One of the inferences that could be drawn from his analysis is that the Melbourne auditors were also among the best equipped to tackle the consolidation problem.

TABLE 7.2

Frequency Distributions: Auditors Consolidators (Non-Consolidators)

Number of Audits	Number of Audit Firms	Totals
1	24 (24)	24 (24)
2	4 (2)	8 (4)
3	2 (0)	6 (0)
4	1 (1)	4 (4)
Totals	31 (27)	42*(32)*

*Includes double counting of 2 joint audits in each group.

TABLE 7.3

Distribution of Multiple Audit Firms

Audit Firm	Consolidators	(Non-Consolidators)
Parsons Anderson & Co.	4	(1)
Yarwood Vane & Co.	3	(1)
Priestley and Morris	3	(1)
Carruthers Farram & Co.	2	(2)
McDonald Ross & Co.	2	(0)
G.A. Blackett and Lewis	2	(1)
Cooper Bros, Way and Hardie	2	(1)
Smith Johnson & Co.	1	(4)
Starkey and Starkey	1	(2)
Totals	20	13

Table 7.3 and, as indicated, all but one appear in both groups. While the cell sizes in Table 7.3 are too small to allow significance testing, there is a very slight suggestion of an audit firm effect in this subset of the data. The three firms that appear most frequently in the consolidating group appear least frequently in the non-consolidating group; and vice versa. Note that this effect is unrelated to geography or location since all of these firms were Sydney (N.S.W.) based. Note also that none of these firms had established an advocacy position (in either direction) on the matter of consolidation.

Finally, while it is not apparent from the Tables, there were only 2 (4) instances of audit firm changes in the consolidating (non consolidating) groups in the year of consolidation. For the consolidators the 2 switches were to completely new audit firms (one of which was Yarwood Vane); for the non-consolidators each case involved at least one of the original auditors staying on following a change in partnership arrangements.

7.3 TAXATION RELATED INCENTIVES TO CONSOLIDATE

Identifying the possible effects of tax on management's incentive to consolidate over 1930-1960 period is complicated by the multiplicity of taxing authorities, types of taxes and changes therein over this period. Appendix III contains a detailed description of the income tax regime to which listed Australian companies were subject between 1930-1960 and provides the necessary institutional background to the summary provided below. The analysis proceeds in two stages. The first matter investigated is the existence or otherwise of any direct taxation related incentives to consolidate. The second is the indirect relationship that exists between corporate taxation and corporate financial reporting through the effect of the former on the choice of organisational form.

7.3.1 Direct Taxation Related Incentives to Consolidate

Given an income taxation environment of the type described in Appendix III, the question arises as to the incentives, if any, this provided for companies to consolidate? In terms of direct incentives the answer to this question is, with one exception (discussed subsequently) - none. Quite simply, each of the taxes referred to in Appendix III was levied on the separate income of the legal entity deriving that income. It is a fundamental principle of Australian income tax law that the income (losses) of one company cannot be aggregated with the income (losses) of any other i.e., consolidation for taxation purposes is not permitted (Gunn, 1948, pp.335-338).[10]

The exception to this rule arises because of the manner in which the special war-time company tax was assessed. As indicated above this tax was levied at an increasing rate (ultimately up to 78 percent) on the amount by which the taxable income exceeded a

---

10. On August 21, 1984 the Federal Treasurer, in his budget speech, foreshadowed the introduction of "group taxation" for the first time. Of the numerous committees and commissions that have reported on taxation in Australia (Warren Kerr 1921-23, Ferguson 1932-34, Spooner 1950-54, Hulme 1954-55, Ligertwood 1959-61 and Asprey 1975) only the Ferguson and Asprey enquiries make any reference to group taxation. The former incorrectly concluded (p.118) that disregarding the special property tax then in force "holding companies have little to gain or lose by aggregation". The latter recommended the adoption of "limited" group taxation - a recommendation which was not acted upon (see also Finn and Payne, 1977, pp.19-20).

"percentage standard". This standard was set ultimately at 5 percent of the capital employed. The starting point for the calculation of capital was defined (War-Time (Company) Tax Assessment Act, Sn.24) as the average paid-up capital, accumulated profits and reserves (excluding current profits) of the company. This figure was adjusted up or down depending upon whether or not the "prescribed values" of any assets exceeded or fell below their book values. The prescribed values of assets were essentially the amount at which they were taken into account for taxation purposes. Intangibles had a prescribed value of zero. Likewise, any funds invested in shares in any other company were to be deducted from capital.[11]

However for the purposes of this tax holding companies had one very important option. Section 17 of the Act provided that:

> A holding company may elect, in the manner and within the time period prescribed, to have all its subsidiary companies treated as branches of the holding company ... and no separate assessment shall be made in respect of any of those subsidiary companies.

Thus during the period 1940-41 to 1945-46 holding companies had the option (for the purposes of the war-time company tax) of "grouping" or taking separate assessments for each subsidiary. The former strategy would bring into the capital base the parent's share of post-acquisition retained earnings and reserves in its subsidiaries (at tax rather than book values) and simultaneously avoid the required deduction from capital of investments in other companies. In other words grouping provided credit for, rather than penalizing, investments in subsidiary companies. Further,

---

11. Correspondingly, dividends in respect of such shareholdings were excluded from the definition of taxable income.

given the progressivity in the tax function the total tax on the mean (or group) rate of return would have been less than the sum of the taxes on the individual companies in the group.

There were thus strong incentives to group, or consolidate, for certain tax purposes; and it is possible that the companies which elected to do so carried the practice through to their external reporting. In this sense there may be a direct "tax effect" on consolidation. The preceding discussion implies:

> H7: Australian holding companies which chose to consolidate for financial years ending June 30, 1941 to June 30, 1946 were more likely to be "grouping" for the purposes of the war-time company tax than those holding companies which chose not to consolidate.

Unfortunately there is no way of directly testing this hypothesis largely because it is not possible, even ex post, to identify those companies which were grouping for tax purposes. Four of the consolidators and 6 of the non-consolidators had "event dates" falling in this 6 year sub-period. A detailed survey of each of their annual reports for each year of the sub-period revealed no mention of any company being subject to the special war-time company tax.

7.3.2(i) Indirect Taxation Related Incentives to Consolidate

With the immediately preceding exception income taxation considerations are unlikely to have been a major determinant of management's decision to consolidate for external purposes. However, it is possible that during those periods in which an element of progression in either the primary or special rates of tax existed such considerations could have influenced management's choice of organisational structure i.e., the number of subsidiaries (rather than divisions) through which the company conducted its operations. For example, both the sliding scale (NSW, 1927-1935) and the step in the tax function (post 1947) provide an incentive for tax minimization/avoidance through multiple incorporations (see also Parsons, 1967, p.22).[12]

To this point attention has been restricted to the influence of income taxes on the choice of organisational form. There is, however, another possible incentive for multiple incorporation in the form of pay-roll tax. The Commonwealth first imposed a pay-roll tax at the rate of 2.5 percent on all wages paid or payable by employers in respect of any period of time subsequent to June 30, 1941.[13] There was a general exemption of $2080 per annum; which had increased by September 1957 to $20,800 per annum - though the rate of tax itself remained at 2.5 percent. As an indication of the relative significance of payroll tax it is worth noting that over the 20 years (1941-61) tax collections from this source ran at an average of 24.4 percent of corporate income taxes - with a low of 18.5 and a high of 31.7 percent.[14]

---

12. Note that tax considerations cannot (over the period of this study) have influenced the form of the subsidiary (public or private). Since the introduction of the private company rate differential (refer Appendix III) it has always been the case that a private company which was the subsidiary of a public company, was taxed as a public company. This choice must have been related to other considerations such as the distribution of control, administrative convenience, or the differential external reporting requirements for public and private companies.

13. The Commonwealth transferred its monopoly over payroll tax to the States in September, 1971 and retained an interest in this area only in so far as certain Federal Territories were concerned (Desiatnik, 1973).

14. Based on the Annual Budget Papers, Consolidated Revenue Fund, 1941-1961.

To the extent that tax considerations (both income and payroll) influenced the choice of organisational structure they may indirectly have fostered a demand for consolidated financial information for other purposes (e.g., performance evaluation and contract monitoring - as argued in Chapter 4). While few would doubt the significance of tax considerations as a determinant of organisational form, evidence on this matter is scarce. This aspect is considered next.

7.3.2 (ii) Evidence

The first holding company operating in Australia is said (Spence, 1949, p.186) to have been Elder Smith and Co. Ltd., which acquired a subsidiary in 1882. Henry Jones Co-operative Ltd (4 subsidiaries) and Howard Smith and Co. Ltd. (2 subsidiaries) became holding companies with the acquisition of their subsidiaries in 1910 and 1912 respectively.[15] However the first major holding company operating in Australia appears to have been The British Tobacco Company (Australia) Ltd. Registered in 1904 in England this company had controlling interests in the 5 leading Australian Companies involved in the manufacture, importing and distribution of tobacco.[16]

---

15. Two large private company groups were set up at around the same time. Carlton and United Breweries Pty. Ltd. was formed in 1907 to takeover five breweries operating in Victoria. Similarly the Southern Star Co. was established in 1908 to takeover 6 companies involved in the manufacture and importing of nails and barbed wire (refer Wilkinson, 1914, Chapters 6 and 7).

16. A decision in the English courts regarding the incidence of taxation led to the formation of an Australian holding company Consolidated Investment Co. Ltd., in 1927. This company's name was changed to the British Tobacco (Australia) Ltd. in 1928 upon listing (refer Appendix II, Case Study No.7).

TABLE 7.4

Growth of the Holding Company Form
N.S.W. and Victoria - Listed Public Companies

Year	Holding Companies: Relative Frequency	Holding Companies: %	Population Surveyed	Reference
1920	6/215	2.79		
1930	45/491	9.16		
1931	42/481	8.73		
1932	42/464	8.83		
1933	43/442	9.73	Jobsons Investment Digest:	
1934	53/455	11.65	N.S.W. and Victorian	
1935	66/465	14.19	Registered Companies	Chapter 2.3
1936	65/471	13.80		
1937	112/496	22.58		
1938	132/507	26.04		
1939	160/511	31.31		
1940	152/419	36.28		
1941	134/420	31.90		
1943	170/417	40.77		
1947	178/387	45.99		
1950	207/387	53.49		
1939	101/288	35.1	Sydney and Melbourne	Goldberg and
1947	146/331	44.1	Stock Exchanges	Hocking (1949)
1945	60/300	20.0	Melbourne Stock	Fitzgerald
1949	200/500	40.0	Exchange	(1950)

It was not until the second half of the 1920's that the holding company form assumed any significance in Australia (Fitzgerald, 1950). Even then it's growth was apparently retarded by the Commonwealth's extra tax on "property income" (Editorial, 1933, p.86), which included (but was not restricted to) inter-company dividends.[17]

Some indication of the growth of the holding company form is available in Table 7.4. The first panel in the Table is based on the same survey sources as described in Chapter 2.3. Once again only companies that could be unambiguously identified as having subsidiaries have been included. The second and third panels are based on surveys conducted by the authors identified therein and are presented for comparative purposes only.

It is apparent from the Table that prior to 1930 the holding company form of organisation was relatively uncommon (up to approximately 3 percent of listed public companies). Consistent with the view expressed in the Editorial referred to above the removal of the Commonwealth's property income tax in financial 1935/36 was followed by a 72 percent increase (calendar 1937) in the number of holding companies in N.S.W. and Victoria.

Between 1937-38 and 1940-41 Commonwealth income taxes increased by over 400 percent (Appendix III, Table 1); though most of this increase occurred in 1940-41. Over this interval there was a 26 percent increase in the number of companies paying

---

17. See also Appendix III, Table 1. This tax ranged over time from 5.0 to 10.0 percent. The editorial went on to observe that some companies had been placed in liquidation or reconstructed in such a manner as to cease to come under the category of holding company.

tax (11,028 to 13,927) but a 473 percent increase in total company income tax revenues ($7.028m to $40.288m).[18] This period also corresponds with one of continued growth in the holding company form - a growth which appears to receive some stimulus from the introduction of pay-roll tax in the 1941-42 income year. Between calendar 1941 and 1943 (i.e., the years immediately preceding and following the introduction of pay-roll tax) the number of holding companies increased by approximately 27 percent (i.e., from 134 to 170, or 32 to 41 percent of listed companies). Consistent with this view, Goldberg and Hocking (1949, p.10) also observe:

> ...a marked tendency in a considerable number of cases for companies which were holding companies in 1939 to increase the number of subsidiary companies which they controlled....

By the end of the war (1947) the number of holding companies had increased to approximately 46 percent of listed public companies, and by 1950 this proportion was in excess of 50 percent. The figures for 1947 and 1950 in Table 7.4 are consistent with the introduction of the step in the function in 1947-48 (Appendix III, Table 2) providing additional stimulus to the multiple incorporation phenomenon.

In summary, the evidence suggests that the holding company form spread rapidly after the removal of the property income tax. In as much as the rate of growth in the holding company form has exceeded that of companies in general immediately following the introduction of both pay-roll taxes and the step in the tax function these taxes appear to have acted as a further stimulant

---

18. Based on figures available in Department of Treasury, Budget, (1937 - 1941), passim.

to the use of this form of organisation. While these tax effects do not provide any direct incentives for management to consolidate, as argued above, it is likely that they increased the demand for consolidated financial information for other purposes - performance evaluation, contract monitoring etc.

7.4 OTHER INFLUENCES

A number of previous studies have hypothesized that large firms are subject to greater government scrutiny and possible wealth transfers than small firms and that to reduce these "political" costs they choose income reducing accounting techniques.[19] Over the time period of this study consolidation was, on average , both an income and asset increasing accounting technique (refer Chapter 6.2). Thus it could be argued that larger firms are less likely to consolidate than smaller firms. However, there are a number of problems with such an argument. First, there is a problem of construct validity i.e., just how good a proxy is firm size for the level of political costs? (Ball and Foster, 1982, p.182). Second, the same prediction is consistent with Verrechia's (1979) theory of market information efficiency - a theory in which political costs play no part. Third, a size variable did not enter the theoretical analysis of Chapter 4. For these reasons the political cost hypothesis is not explicitly pursued here. However, to the extent that political costs are related to either size or industry the profile analysis of Chapter 6.2 indicates that they are unlikely to be an important

---

19. Refer Watts and Zimmerman (1978) and Holthausen and Leftwich (1983).

determinant of the consolidation decision.

In a similar vein it might also be argued that there were a number of significant events over the 1930-1960 period that changed the political environment in which firms operated and hence may have provided an incentive to consolidate. The period opened with the famous Royal Mail case in 1931, the Cohen Committee submitted it's report in 1944 and during the decade of the fifties the accounting profession developed its first "standards".[20] In each instance one matter of concern was holding company disclosure.

The extent to which these events may have been responsible for the adoption of consolidated financial reporting is a moot point. Consolidation was a relatively widespread practice before either Cohen or the profession exhibited concern with this issue. In contrast, the Royal Mail case preceded extensive reliance on either consolidated reporting or the holding company form in Australia. This case may have resulted in changes in the contracting practices and information requirements of creditors or in a revision of auditor attitudes toward holding company disclosure. However these propositions are not directly testable and are not considered further here.

7.5 SUMMARY

The hypotheses developed above are not mututally exclusive - either of each other or of those developed in Chapter 4. While

---

20. The impact of these events on the evolution of accounting and reporting requirements/practices in both the U.K. and Australia is reviewed in Walker (1977), Evans (1974) and Gibson (1971).

these hypotheses are, in principle, testable it is also the case that powerful tests of them are not possible largely due to data availabilty considerations. With this caveat in mind, the analysis presented here reveals no evidence of overseas or auditor-advocate effects in the data. Likewise there is little evidence of a direct tax effect on the decision to consolidate. However, to the extent that changes in the tax system promoted the growth of the holding company form it can be argued that tax had an indirect effect on the consolidation phenomenon.

CHAPTER 8

SYNTHESIS AND CONCLUSIONS

This study commences with the observation (Chapter 2) that many Australian companies adopted what was by historical standards a relatively complex, costly and detailed form of financial disclosure/reporting (consolidated financial reporting) in the absence of any legal or institutional requirements for them to do so. It also observes (Chapter 3) that the widespread adoption of this form of reporting was correlated with the removal of capital issues controls and the development of a market for public debt. It then asks the question - why?

The basic argument (Chapter 4) is that the demand for this form of reporting evolved as a result of contracting procedures aimed at firm value maximization by preventing (or facilitating the detection of) opportunistic behaviour by managers. That is, consolidation evolved out of the necessity for monitoring performance under, or compliance with, the contracts into which the firm had entered and in particular those written between the firm and it's suppliers of debt and equity capital.

The evidence presented in this study (Chapter 6) supports a number of general conclusions. Consolidation was more likely to be adopted in situations in which cross-guarantees between related corporations were present and/or those in which management's share of a firm's equity was relatively small. The likelihood of consolidation was also a function of the number and type of subsidiaries. While these circumstances may be characterized as potentially high agency cost situations, ex post opportunism is shown to be an unlikely explanation for the results.

With the exception of the separation of ownership from control the relative significance of these factors was time dependent. While early consolidators could be characterized as having more subsidiaries than non-consolidators this difference disappeared following the introduction of taxation incentives for multiple incorporation in the early 1950s. Similarly during the period in which Government Capital Issues Controls effectively substituted for contractual constraints on leverage, consolidators/non-consolidators did not differ on this dimension. Yet they did so both prior to the introduction, and subsequent to the removal, of these controls.

The contracting cost variables overwhelmed all others in terms of explanatory power - though it is also apparent that they were not the sole determinant of management's choice of reporting mechanism. In this regard there was little evidence of systematic overseas, taxation, or auditor-advocate effects in the data. However, to the extent that taxation changes promoted the growth of the holding company form, tax may be said to have had an indirect effect on the demand for consolidated financial statements. To the extent that poli-tical costs may be related to either size or industry they too are ruled out as explanatory variables. Regulation and/ or institutional requirements were, of course, ruled out by the sample selection criteria. In contrast, a public/ private debt dichotomy provided modest explanatory power.

There are a number of differences between this and prior studies. First, an ex ante (cf., ex post) perspective is adopted.

This framework allows for the possibility that firms with no debt (or debt constraints) might consolidate, as might firms that are not anywhere near a debt constraint (assuming one exists).

Second, it is argued that the presence of cross-guarantees will be an important determinant of management's decision to consolidate. A detailed analysis of the incentive structure confronting both borrowers and lenders in group lending situations, their respective legal positions, and financial contracting practices in Australia leads to the conclusion that the presence of cross-guarantees is related to both the degree of ownership of subsidiaries and the ratio of secured debt to assets-in-place in the borrowing corporation. These variables may be contrasted with the conventional leverage ratio (Debt/Equity) that is typically employed as a proxy for the agency costs of debt in such studies. Indeed, in the present study the firms do not differ along this conventionally examined dimension.

Third, the costs of monitoring are typically handled as omitted variables in accounting choice studies.[1] As Chapter 4.3 indicates the nature of the consolidation process is such that the costs associated with it can be expected to behave in a reasonably predictable manner and, in particular, they are likely to be increasing in the number of subsidiaries. This factor is explicitly incorporated into the analysis of when management will consolidate and the evidence presented in Chapter 6 is consistent with its hypothesized effects.

---

1. Equivalently, it is assumed that there is no cross-sectional or time-series variation in this factor (refer Leftwich, Watts and Zimmerman, 1981, p.60).

The argument and evidence presented in this thesis also support the view that the adoption of consolidated financial reporting was the logical outcome of a complex series of changes in the environment in which firms were operating - as described below.

Chapter 7.3 and Appendix III document the taxation environment in which Australian firms operated between 1930 and 1962. Chapter 7.3.2 documents, for the first time, a relationship between changes in this environment and the rapid growth of the holding company form of organisation in the latter half of the 1930s and the early 1940s. Chapter 3 documents a subsequent change in the capital markets in which these firms competed and a relationship between this change and the spread of consolidated reporting.

Fundamental changes in both the way in which firms organise, and the markets in which they compete for capital, would be accompanied by changes in the types of opportunistic behaviour in which management could engage. They are also likely to lead to increasingly complex capital structures (e.g., multiple borrowers, multiple sources of funds and multiple "securities" given within the group); thus compounding this problem. Changes in the nature of the financial contracts written between the firm and its suppliers could be expected to ensue. These, in turn, are likely to imply a change in the optimal form of financial reporting for monitoring performance under the contracts. In particular, it is argued that both the contracts and the monitoring device (financial reports) could be expected to try to undo the effects of any taxation induced changes in organisational structure. The solutions to these problems appear to have been cross-guarantees (supported by constraints defined over the borrowing corporation and its guarantors) and consolidated financial statements respectively.

Thus while there is an important sense in which it can be maintained that changes in contracting or agency cost variables were responsible for changes in management's reporting practices, it is also important to realize that the changes in these variables were simply manifestations of changes in the underlying economic/legal environment in which firms operated.

APPENDIX I

Reporting Histories of Australian Holding Companies 1930-40

The following Table contains the reporting histories of those companies that could be identified from Jobson's Investment Digest as adopting some form of disclosure regarding their "investment in subsidiaries" over the period 1930-1940 inclusive. Three types of disclosure have been delineated:

x separate subsidiary statements

xx aggregate (combined) financial statements of subsidiaries

xxx consolidated financial statements.

The nature of the various types of disclosure was discussed in Chapter 2.1.2.

These data form the basis for the summary statistics reported in Table 2.1. One caveat is warranted. As indicated above these companies were initially identified as "disclosers" from a survey of Jobson's. However, a number of cross-checks indicated that Jobson's (and both the Melbourne Record and the Sydney Gazette) occassionally aggregated parent and subsidiary accounts for review purposes when the company's annual accounts contained no such aggregation or combination. As a consequence, each company's reporting behaviour has been cross-checked to original records on file at either the Sydney or Melbourne Stock Exchanges. Note finally that the Table contains a company's history since the first disclosure regarding its subsidiaries. The absence of a prior history can mean one of two things - either the company has been listed for some time but has presented only parent company financial statements or the company has just been listed (the former was the most common occurence).

APPENDIX I
Reporting Histories of Australian Holding Companies 1930-40

Name	State	1930	1931	1932	1933	1934	1935	1936	1937	1938	1939	1940	Comments[1]
General Industries Ltd	NSW	xx	xx	xx	xx	xx	xx	xx	xx	xx	xx	xx	
Marshalls Ltd	VIC	x	x	x	x'	x	x	x	-	-	-	-	Wound up 1937
Lincoln Mills (Australia) Ltd	VIC	xx	xx	xxx	xxx	xxx	xxx	xxx	xxx	xxx	xxx	x	Case Study No.1 subs. wound up 1940
R. White and Son Ltd	VIC	x	x	-	-	-	-	-	-	-	-	-	Wound up 1932
Toledo-Berkel (Australia) Ltd	VIC	x	x	x	x	x	x	x	x	x	xxx	xxx	
United Provisions Ltd	VIC	xx	xx	xx	xx	xx	xx	xx	xx	xx	xxx	xxx	
Marcus Clark (Victoria) Ltd	VIC	x	x	x	x	x	x	x	x	x	x	x	
Hoyts Theatres Ltd	VIC		xxx	xxx	xxx	xxx	xxx	xxx	xxx	xxx	xxx	xxx	Case Study No.2
Mayne Nickless (Australia) Ltd	VIC	x	x	x	x	x	-	-	-	-	-	-	Reconstructed as single company
Drug Houses of Australia Ltd	VIC		xx	xx	xx	xx	xx	xx	xx	xx	xxx	xxx	
Associated Newspapers Ltd	NSW		xx	-	x	x	x	x	-	-	-	-	Subs in liquidation 1937
British Tobacco (Australia) Ltd	VIC				x	x	x	x	xxx	xxx	xxx	xxx	Case Study No.7
Sydney Ferries Ltd	NSW					x	x	x	x	x	x	x	
Dunlop Perdriau Rubber Coy Ltd	VIC						xxx	xxx	xxx	xxx	xxx	xxx	Case Study No.4
Whakatane Paper Mills Ltd	NSW						xxx	xxx	xxx	xxx	xxx	xxx	Case Study No.5
Electricity Meter and Allied Industries Ltd	NSW					xx	xx	xx	xx	xx	xx	xx	
Associated Investments Ltd	VIC								xx	xx	xxx	xxx	
Felt and Textiles of Australia Ltd	NSW								xxx	xxx	xxx	xxx	Case Study No.6
Carlton Brewery Ltd	VIC										xxx	xxx	
Carrier Australasia Ltd	NSW								xx	xx	xx	xx	
Brooklands Accessories Ltd	VIC									x	x	x	
Beaurepaire Investments Ltd	VIC									x	x	x	

Name	State	1930	1931	1932	1933	1934	1935	1936	1937	1938	1939	1940	Comments
Williams Atkins Holdings Ltd	NSW									x	x	x	
Schute Bell Badgery & Lumby Ltd	NSW								xxx	x	x	x	Case Study No.8 no explanation given for change
McIlrath's Holdings Ltd	NSW									xx	xx	xx	
Claude Neon Industries Ltd	VIC										xxx	xxx	
Allied Bruce Small Ltd	VIC								xx	xx	xxx	xxx	
McEwans Ltd	VIC									x	x	x	
Consolidated Fibre Products Ltd	VIC									xxx	xxx	xxx	Case Study No.10
Bradford Cotton Mills	NSW										xxx	xxx	Case Study No.11
Geo. W. Kelly & Lewis Ltd	VIC										xxx	xxx	
Allied Motor Interests Ltd	VIC										xxx	xxx	
Holeproof Ltd	VIC										xxx	xxx	
Huddart Parker Ltd	VIC										xxx	xxx	
Australian Consolidated Industries Ltd	VIC											xxx	
Swallow and Ariell Ltd	VIC											xxx	
Sutex Ltd	VIC											xxx	
Melbourne Cooperative Brewery Ltd	VIC											xxx	
Yarra Falls Ltd	VIC											xxx	
Hume Pipe Coy (Australia) Ltd	VIC										xxx	xxx	
Electronic Industries Ltd	VIC											xxx	
Gas Supply Coy of Victoria	VIC											xxx	
A.W. Allen Ltd	VIC											xxx	
Henry Berry and Company (Australasia) Ltd	VIC											xxx	
New Northcote Bricks Ltd	VIC											xxx	

Name	State	1930	1931	1932	1933	1934	1935	1936	1937	1938	1939	1940	Comments
Prestige Ltd	VIC											xxx	
Melbourne Steamship Co. Ltd	VIC										xxx	xxx	
Broken Hill Pty. Co. Ltd	VIC										xxx	xxx	
Griffith Bros Ltd	VIC											xxx	
Repco Ltd	VIC									xxx	xxx	xxx	Case Study No.9
Geo. Pizzey & Son Ltd	VIC											xxx	
Gippsland & Northern Cooperative Ltd	VIC											xxx	
Zinc Investments Ltd	VIC											xxx	
Imperial Chemical Industries of Australia & New Zealand Ltd	VIC										xxx	xxx	
Carlton and United Breweries	VIC										xxx	xxx	
Johns and Waygood Ltd	VIC										xxx	xxx	
Myer Emporium Ltd	VIC										xxx	xxx	
Woolworths Ltd	NSW									xx	xx	xx	
Adelaide Motors Ltd	SA					xxx	xxx	xxx	xxx	xxx	xxx	xxx	Case Study No.3
Ellis Caterers Ltd	SA									xxx	xxx	xxx	

Legend: x Separate Subsidiary Statements

xx Aggregate (Combined) Statements of Subsidiaries

xxx Consolidated Financial Statements

Note: 1 Reference to Case Studies refers to Appendix III

APPENDIX II

Case Studies - N.S.W. Consolidators prior to 1941 Stock Exchange Requirement and Victorian Consolidators prior to 1938 Act

This Appendix incorporates the case histories of the first 11 listed public companies to adopt the consolidated form of financial reporting in the absence of any institutional requirements for them to do so. The companies were identified from the data in Appendix I, Table I. They have been prepared in accordance with the procedure laid out in Chapter 5.3.1. Certain regularities are apparent and these, as well as data on those factors that may be related to the consolidation phenomena (as hypothesized in Chapters 4 and 7), are summarized in Table 1.

The column vectors in the Table each refer to a specific case. The row vectors indicate the presence or otherwise of a change in the relevant factor in the financial year immediately preceding the release of consolidated accounts. The factors are defined as follows:

Operating structure - refers to the creation of, or an increase in, the number of subsidiaries or a move from using divisions to using subsidiaries;

Ownership structure - refers to the issue of ordinary or preference shares (i.e., a change in distribution of ownership most often associated with the firm going "public");

Management structure- refers to a change in the Board of Directors[1];

Contract structure - refers to the presence or otherwise of any of a variety of contracts into which the firm may have entered for the first time;

---

1. Note that changes in either ownership or management structure do not necessarily imply a change in the distribution of "control" in the organisation. Indeed, there was only one instance (Case No.1) in which control changed hands.

TABLE 1

Summary of Case Studies

Case Number/Year Associated Event - Changes in:	1 1931	2 1932	3 1934	4 1935	5 1936	6 1937	7 1937	8 1937	9 1938	10 1938	11 1939
Operating Structure	/	/			/	/		/			/
Ownership Structure											
. pref. shares	/				/					/	
. ord. shares	/					/		/	/		/
Management Structure	/			/			/				
Contract Structure											
. Articles								/		/	
. Management Compensation						/					
. Cross-guarantees	/	/	/			/					/
. Other			/								
Auditors	/										
Overseas Influences	/			/							
Other							/				/

Auditors	-	refers to a change in Auditors;
Overseas influences	-	refers to the presence or otherwise of substantial overseas shareholdings in the firm;
Other	-	refers to the presence of miscellaneous factors that may be of relevance - details appear in relevant case study.

Table 1 reveals that in general terms consolidation followed closely (8/11 instances) a change in the underlying contracts into which the firm had entered. In some instances more than one such contract may have changed. For example, there were 5 instances of the creation of cross-guarantees, 1 of the writing of a management compensation plan tied to "group" profits, 2 in which articles of association were modified and 1 in which consolidation followed the writing of an agreement with preference shareholders relating to participation in "excess" profits. Table 1 also reveals that changes in the firm's underlying contractual structure were in the majority of cases preceded by either, or both, a change in the firm's operating (5/7) or ownership (5/7) structure.

Two cases (4 and 7) stand out as having experienced no changes in operating, ownership or contract structures in the year preceding consolidation. The first N.S.W. company to consolidate (Case No.4, Dunlop) did so a number of years after it acquired its first major subsidiary and after it had become associated with the English company of the same name. However, it consolidated very shortly after its English associate had done so and following significant management changes - including the appointment of a new managing director with overseas experience. Similarly, British Tobacco (Case No.7) which at one stage had a Board of Directors opposed to consolidation, eventually consolidated - but after significant changes in the Board and following shareholder pressure at earlier annual general meetings.

The one instance of a change in auditors (Case No.1, Hoyts) is noticeable since it resulted in a well known opponent of consolidation (J.V.M. Wood) sharing responsibility for the audit with another firm (Yarwood Vane). However, as can be seen from the Table, this was just one of many concurrent events for this firm.

A number of other features of Table 1 warrant brief comment. First, one industry (textiles) is represented three times - Cases 1,6, and 11. The case histories reveal that these companies appeared to have weathered the depression relatively well and that the second half of the 1930s was one of considerable potential for the industry. Indeed each of these companies consolidated just prior to approaching the market for growth capital. Second, the case studies indicate that the principal source of long-term capital for all of the firms was, with one exception, either a bank overdraft or a new issue of shares (either ordinary or preference).[2] Further in each instance (bar one) that an overdraft existed it was possible to establish that contingent liabilities under guarantees existed (6/7).[3] Third, while the companies Articles of Association typically provide that "the

---

2. Note this trend is consistent with that reported in Chapter 3 for this time period. The exception was Case No.1, Hoyts which relied heavily on U.S. parent company loans and an issue of debentures to the public by one of its subsidiaries.

3. Case No.4 had both overdraft and cross-guarantees in place for some years. Hence it is included in this figure, but not in Table 1, where the emphasis is on changes in contract structures.

remuneration of a Managing Director shall from time to time be fixed by the Directors and may be by way of fixed salary or commission or participation in profits or by any or all of these modes", in only one instance (Case No.6, Felt and Textiles) was evidence of an explicit management compensation plan tied to group earnings detected. Finally, none of the Articles examined contained a borrowing restriction of the type referred to in Chapter 4.2.

Summary

The qualitative evidence contained in this Appendix and suggests the following general conclusion. The majority of Australia's first (i.e., the pre-regulation) consolidators were experiencing (or had just experienced) some form of structural change - either operating, ownership or management - at the time they elected to consolidate. These structural changes were, in the majority of cases, accompanied by corresponding changes in the underlying contract structure of the firm (most often cross-guarantees). Indeed, in only two instances (Cases 4 and 7) were such changes entirely absent. However, while such changes are consistent with the arguments developed in Chapter 4 and with the evidence presented in Chapter 6, the absence of a control group of companies cautions against heavy reliance on these results.

CASE STUDY NO.1

Hoyts Theatres Ltd

Background

This company was incorporated in Victoria in November 1926 to takeover as going concerns the Hoyts Group of Theatres (operated by 3 separate proprietary companies and numbering over 20) and the J.C. Williamson Group of Theatres (operated by 6 separate proprietary companies and numbering over 50). The company also acquired controlling interests in 3 other proprietary companies. To provide funds for expansion the company issued preference shares to the public in November 1926. Shortly thereafter the company acquired controlling interests in another 4 proprietaries - bringing the number of theatres under its control to in excess of 100. Further preference issues and debt financing (mortgage loans) provided capital for continued expansion and development. In 1929 a new subsidiary was set up in N.S.W. funded jointly by parent company equity and a £100,000 public debenture issue. With the onset of the depression, the company (already heavily in debt and subject to high property and entertainment taxes) was in severe financial distress. During 1930-31 Fox Film Corporation (a U.S. company) provided such financial accommodation as was necessary and in addition acquired substantial (i.e., controlling) holdings of both ordinary and preference shares. The 1931 annual report reveals a substantial reorganization followed. Four of the companies five founding directors and, until this time principal ordinary shareholders, were removed from the Board - including the joint managing directors. Also, for the first time joint auditors were appointed at the annual general meeting (J.V.M. Wood; Starkey and Starkey). The former had until this time been the sole auditor.[1]

In 1932 a new company was formed (General Theatres Corporation of Australasia Ltd) to takeover the city theatres of Hoyts and its principal opposition, Greater Union Theatres, for a period of five years. The new company was owned and controlled equally by the two companies and the agreement came into effect in January 1933. The suburban and country theatres were unaffected by this arrangement and remained under the control of the Board.

In 1934 the company drew up an agreement to reconcile the interests of all classes of shareholders. Preference shareholders agreed to dividend reductions and in order to pay off the arrears of dividends the company agreed that out of profits a dividend at the reduced rate would be paid; and out of any surplus of profits thereafter a sum of £10,000 (or as much as was left) was to be paid off the arrears. Provision was made for the appointment of 2 directors to represent the interests of the A and B preference shareholders. The agreement also provided that capital losses on the then existing assets should not be a charge on the profits of the company.

The latter clause resulted in accumulated losses of a capital nature being carried forwarded in a "Depleted Assets Account" for many years - resulting finally in a major reduction in capital in 1937 (£1 to 1/-). Thereafter the company continued to trade profitably.

---

1. Chapter 4.2 identifies Wood as a prominent Melbourne accountant who opposed consolidation.

Operating Structure

The parent operated from its inception primarily (though not entirely) as the holding company for a large and growing group of companies. Six months prior to its first consolidated accounts in 1933 the company hired off a substantial portion of its assets (i.e., its city theatres) into another operating subsidiary. Thereafter its structure remained relatively stable for many years.

Ownership Structure

At inception the company was owned and managed basically by its two founding managing directors, who had been the principal shareholders in the amalgamating groups. 'A' preference shares were offered to the public; 'B' and 'C' preference shares were issued in satisfaction of the merger. The former were taken up by several hundred shareholders. Some 500,000 £1 fully paid ordinary shares issued at the same time were held largely by the joint managing directors. During 1930-31 (as indicated above) control of the corporation shifted into the hands of the Fox Corporation of America. The ordinary share remained in their hands and unlisted.

Management

During 1930-31 4 of the original 5 founding directors resigned (refer above). The restructured board included the remaining member of the original Directorate (J.H. Tait), a representative of preference shareholders (G. Robinson) and four new (Fox) appointments viz:

S.S. Crick - Chairman of Directors
C.E. Munro - Managing Director
C. Minter - Director
B. Barron - Director

Financial Reporting

The company's accounts for the financial year ending in June 1933 were released in October. They were accompanied by an unaudited consolidated balance sheet. However, since the 1931 annual general meeting the company had adopted a policy of providing a "supplementary" consolidated balance sheet to shareholders in attendance at the annual general meeting.

Contracts in force

Debt: The company's 1931 financial statements disclose for the first time contingent liabilities under various contracts and in respect of guarantees to Banks for advances to Subsidiary Companies; also in respect of advances on mortgage to subsidiary companies and balances due under contracts of sale and agreements by subsidiary companies.

Equity: No evidence available.

Management: No evidence available.

Summary

In this case consolidation follows closely substantive changes in:

(i) the firm's operating structure,
(ii) the distribution of both ownership and control (involving an overseas parent),
(iii) the extension of cross-guarantees, and
(iv) a change in auditors.

Principal References

Sydney Stock Exchange Reference: H19 (Hoyts Theatres Ltd)

Sydney Stock Exchange Reference: H3 (Hoyts Theatres (NSW) Ltd).

CASE STUDY NO.2

Lincoln Mills (Australia) Ltd

Background

This company was incorporated in Victoria in March 1926 following a reconstruction of a company of the same name which had been set up four years earlier to acquire all of the issued capital of Lincoln Spinning Mills Pty. Ltd and Lincoln Knitting Mills Pty Ltd; but had encountered serious difficulties. Results were disappointing for the first three years but in 1929 the operating companies entered a period of prosperity that was maintained even during the depression. The group reorganized in July 1931. Thereafter the parent, which until this time had operated purely as a holding company, undertook the distribution of all of the production of its subsidiaries. The following years were profitable but, with the object of reducing operating expenses, the two subsidiaries were wound up in December 1939 and their assets and operations were taken over by the parent.

Operating Structure

From March 1926 until December 1939 the groups structure was as follows:

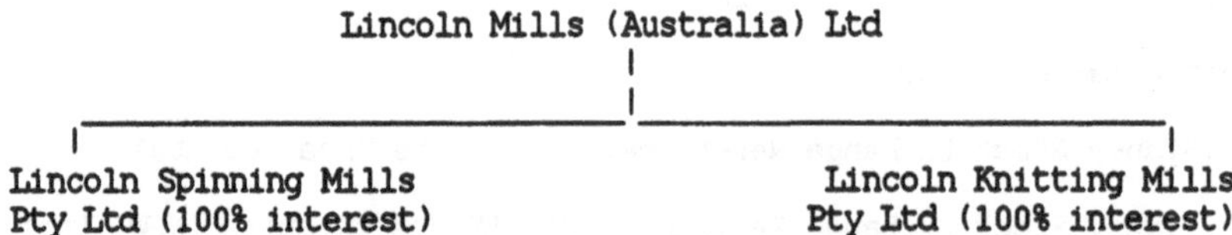

In July 1931 the holding company become a distributing (i.e., operating) company. In December 1939 the subsidiaries were wound up (refer above).

Ownership

Prior to the 1926 reorganization issued capital stood as 402,631 £1 fully paid ordinary shares and 400,000 £1 fully paid 9% cumulative preference shares. Following this reorganization the capital stood as

402,631 4/- fully paid ordinary shares and
400,000 £1 fully paid 9% cumulative preference shares.

The preference shares were granted listing in September 1926. The ordinary shares were not granted quotation (until 1951) because:

> ...they are held in very few hands, an are not sufficiently distributed to warrant it. In any case their official listing has not been asked for.
> (Correspondence, M.S.E., 23.6.26)

Management

At the time of consolidation (June 1932) the company was managed by 3 directors (qualification 1,000 shares) viz.[1]:

J. Fox	-	Chairman of Directors		
		Personal Holdings	1,000	ord. shares
		Holdings in name of Fox	37,130 (9.22%)	ord. shares
J. Kellett	-	General Manager and Director		
		Personal Holdings	6,527 (1.62%)	ord. shares
E.T.H. Richardson	-	Director		
		Personal Holdings	3,000 (0.75%)	ord. shares
J.M. Gillespie	-	Director		
		Personal Holdings	1,000 (0.25%)	ord. shares

The size of the board was increased to five with the addition of a Mr. R.S. Fox at the annual general meeting in 1933.

1. Figures are approximate and based on shareholders lists as at May 1951 prior to the listing of the ordinary shares.

Financial Reporting

From June 1926 to June 1931 the company presented parent company accounts and the combined accounts of the two operating subsidiaries. However, the Directors report for 1932 indicates that the corporate reorganization of July 1931:

> ...has necessitated alterations in the form of the accounts submitted to you; and your Directors have taken the opportunity to supply more detailed information than hitherto, which they hope will be appreciated by shareholders. In this connection attention is particularly drawn to the statement showing the Assets and Liabilities of the Company and its two subsidiaries combined.

That is, the accounts were consolidated financial statements. The consolidated balance sheet was audited.

Contracts in force

Debt: Guarantees in favour of the Bank of New Zealand covering indebtedness of both subsidiaries were disclosed in the 1932 accounts (but not at any time before or after).

Management: No evidence available.

Equity: The articles were those of the pre-1926 company (not observable). In response to a query from the Sydney Exchange (Correspondence 20.5.26) the secretary of the Melbourne Exchange (Correspondence 23.6.26) replied:

> This is a holding company, but as it is a reconstruction of a Company that was listed upon the Stock Exchange prior to the introduction of the Rule prescribing disclosure of the subsidiary Company's accounts, and as many thousands of the shares have been sold through the Stock Exchange, my Committee consider that the Company should be reinstated upon the list without any obligations additional to those which were imposed upon the original company.

Summary

In this case consolidation follows closely substantive changes in:

(i) the firm's operating structure and

(ii) the extension of cross-guarantees.

Principal References

Sydney Stock Exchange Reference : L3

Correspondence, Melbourne Stock Exchange: 23 June, 1926

Correspondence, Sydney Stock Exchange : 20 May, 1926

CASE STUDY NO.3

Adelaide Motors Ltd

Background

The company was formed in South Australia in June 1922 to takeover the South Australian franchise of Fiat cars; at that time one of the most popular vehicles in Australia. In both 1924 and 1926 the company made preference issues to finance expansion. In 1930 further ordinary shares were issued and the company hived off some of its departments into two newly formed and wholly-owned operating subsidiaries. Hit hard by the depression the company was unable to pay its preference dividends. However in August 1934 the Directors reported that they had finalized an agreement with the preference shareholders whereby they agreed to both (a) forego their 1931-1933 dividends and (b) a modification of their rights. The latter provided for the payment of a 5 percent cumulative preferential dividend annually with a participating right to a further 3 percent in any year in which profits were sufficient to pay 5 percent on ordinary and preference shares and still leave a surplus available for distribution. The first such dividend occurred in financial 1937.

Between 1934 and the onset of World War II conditions improved for the company. However with the loss of supplies that ensued the company accumulated large cash balances, resulting in a return of capital in 1943/44. The company was taken over in July 1955 by Adelaide Motors Investments Ltd.

Operating Structure

As indicated above in 1930 the company formed 2 wholly owned subsidiaries.

Ownership and Management

Ownership:	not determinable but both ordinary and preference shares were listed in Adelaide and Melbourne.
Management: (1935-1955)	F.S. Mann, Director L.M. Anderson, Managing Director R.H. Martin, Chairman of Directors

Financial Reporting

The company's accounts for the financial year ending June 30, 1934 were released in August 1934. They contained an unaudited consolidated balance sheet of the group with separate disclosures relating to the profitability of each subsidiary.

Contracts in force

Debt:	1934 Balance Sheets reveal that both the parent and subsidiary companies were indebted to the E.S. & A. Bank and that there were, in respect of this indebtedness, contingent liabilities under guarantees.
Equity:	The agreement with preference shareholders completed in financial 1934 and described above.
Management:	No evidence available.

Summary

The company appears to have "consolidated" in the year in which the agreement with preference shareholders regarding participation in profits (as defined) was completed. At the same time it is apparent that cross-guarantees exist.

Principal Reference

Sydney Stock Exchange Reference: A 60 A

CASE STUDY NO.4

Dunlop Predriau Rubber Co. Ltd

Background

Though incorporated in Victoria in August 1920 as Dunlop Rubber Australasia Ltd this company's predecessor was first registered in 1899 to acquire the Australasian rights to exploit Dunlop's (England) newly invented tyre. Between 1920 and 1927 the company experienced modest growth. However by 1927 it was experiencing heavy competition, particularly from a newly established company in N.S.W. which was backed by the Goodyear Company of America - one of the largest rubber companies in the world. With this in mind the Directors of Dunlop Australasia entered into an agreement with the Dunlop Rubber Co. Ltd of England in which in return for unrestricted access to the U.K. company's technical expertise and skills (and other benefits) the Australian company issued 500,000 £1 shares at 25/- with an option for 4 years over another 500,000 at 30/-. In addition the U.K. company received the right to appoint 3 Directors - though it could not vote its shares in respect of any of the remaining Directorships. Further the shares could not be sold for 10 years without the approval of the Australian company and in this event the Australian shareholders were to have first right of refusal.

The company continued to prosper and in 1929 completed a merger with Perdriau Rubber Co. Ltd. - resulting in a change in company name. In the same year it also acquired a controlling interest in Barnett Glass Rubber Co. Ltd. It was not until 1936 that the company started to expand again. By 1960 it was the holding company for a large and diversified group of 11 companies.

Operating Structure

With the disposal of its New Zealand operation to Dunlop (U.K.) in 1928 the 1929 acquisition of Barnett Glass became the Australian company's principal subsidiary. The subsidiary was wholly-owned (with the exception of its preference shares).

Ownership

When the company was incorporated in 1920 its paid up capital was comprised of:

200,000 £1 10% cumulative preference shares
90,000 £1 10% second cumulative preference shares
230,000 £1 10% third cumulative preference shares
600,000 £1 ordinary shares

At the time of consolidation in 1935 it had become:

930,000 £1 10% cumulative preference shares
3,765,655 £1 ordinary shares.

Both classes of shares (with the exception of those issued to Dunlop U.K.) were granted quotation and were widely held.

Management

In 1927 the company was managed by 5 directors. Following the 1929 merger the number had been increased to a maximum of 15 structured as follows:

5 Technical directors with service agreements running from 6 to 10 years (2 of these 5 to be managing directors),

3 Nominees of the English Company, and

7 Directors to be subject to rotation in the usual way.

In 1929 15 such Directors were appointed. This number was reduced to 9 in 1935, all of whom had been Directors in 1929. During 1934-35 the joint managing directors retired and a new manager with experience in the U.K., the U.S.A. and Canada was appointed.

Financial Reporting

The company's accounts for the financial year ending June 1935 were released in September and included a set of consolidated financial statements (i.e., balance sheet and income statement). Only the consolidated balance sheet was audited. The company also adopted equity accounting in the parent company accounts in this financial year.[1]

Contracts in force

Debt:	Contingent liabilities under guarantees had existed for some years.
Equity:	Articles of Association, para.123-128 require only a profit and loss account and a balance sheet of the company.
Management:	Service agreements in force; contents not ascertainable.

Summary

This company consolidates a number of years after it acquires its first major subsidiary and its English connections. However it consolidates less than two years after the English company does so (refer Chapter 2.3 footnote 15, infra); and in a year of substantial management changes (including the managing director).

Principal References

Dunlop Rubber Company of Australasia Ltd

Correspondence	: 13 February, 1929
Circular to Shareholders	: 15 August, 1929
Proceedings of General Meeting	: 23 and 25 August, 1929

Sydney Stock Exchange Reference : D9

Melbourne Stock Exchange Official Record: September, 1935, p.445.

1. The parent (and group) accounts still reflected a drop in profits of greater than 50 percent.

CASE STUDY NO.5

Whakatane Paper Mills Ltd

Background

Incorporated in N.S.W. in 1925 as Timberlands Ltd., this company was set up to develop the pulp and paper industry in New Zealand. It undertook to plant the land, maintain the forest, enter into production and arrange for the sale of the timber. Following an agreement with bondholders in 1935 the company converted its bonds into equity capital and its name was changed to Whakatane Paper Mills Ltd. Additional development funds were soon required and this need was satisfied by the issue of 75,711 £1 ordinary shares and 74,128 £1 8% "A" cumulative participating preference shares in financial 1936. Only the latter were listed. During financial 1937 some £73,547 of secured debenture stock (the bulk of which was to mature in December 1938) was issued. This capital was rolled over with a similar debenture issue of £150,000 early in financial 1939. The company did not commence commercial production until July 1939, at which time the Sydney head office was moved to Whakatane, New Zealand.

Operating Structure

As part of the 1935 reorganization the company's operations where divided up into those of the holding company and four wholly-owned New Zealand operating subsidiaries.

Ownership Structure

Just prior to the company's application for listing its paid up capital was comprised of:

1,325,586 fully paid £1 ordinary shares
515,832 partly paid £1 ordinary shares
26,000 fully paid £1 8% cumulative preference shares
28,000 partly paid £1 8% cumulative preference shares

An issue of 74,128 partly paid £1 7% cumulative participating preference shares was subsequently listed. While specific details of the distribution of ownership are not available the company stated (Prospectus, August 1935) that it had, at that time, approximately 12,000 shareholders.

Management

As at June 1936 the company was run by 13 Directors - 8 of whom were N.Z. based (including the Managing Director); and of these 5 had been appointed to represented the converted bondholders. The remaining three directors (including the Chairman of Directors) were Sydney based.

Financial Reporting

The company's first public accounts were released in November 1936. They took the form of an audited consolidated balance sheet for the year ending June, 1936. A comparative consolidated balance sheet for the previous year was made available. Since the company did not operate commercially until 1939 all expenditures prior to this point had been capitalized and no profit and loss accounts were presented. Parent company financial statements did not accompany the consolidated balance sheet.

Contracts in force

No details available as Stock Exchanges files very incomplete.

Summary

In this case consolidation follows closely a change in the company's operating structure and it precedes a number of substantial approaches to the market for debt capital. In this respect it is worth noting (a) the only security for such loans was property, plant, equipment and standing timber in the N.Z.

operating subsidiaries, and (b) the notes to the consolidated balance sheets reveal extensive advances from the parent company to each of its subsidiaries (i.e., substantial "on-lending").

Principal References

Whakatane Paper Mills Ltd.:	Prospectus (August 1935)
Sydney Stock Exchange Reference:	M80
The "Wildcat Monthly":	6 June, 1936, p.245.

CASE STUDY NO.6

Felt and Textiles of Australia Ltd.

Background:

The company was registered in N.S.W. as Sydney Felt and Textiles Ltd. in 1921 with a capital of 6000 £1 fully paid ordinary shares and a local sphere of operations. The company pioneered the manufacture of felted piece goods in Australia. It expanded steadily, acquired its first subsidiary (Federal Felters Pty. Ltd.) in 1931, and by the time it applied for listing in April, 1937 it was the centre of a large group of associated concerns operating throughout Australia, New Zealand and South Africa.

Operating Structure

The company's decision to list followed a year of rapid expansion and management forecasts of future growth. The firm's structure at the time of listing is indicated in Figure 1. The company moved into "slippers" early in 1937 with the acquisition of existing businesses in South Africa and New Zealand. This move followed an earlier one into "wooltops" and "carpet" with the simultaneous establishment of Federal Felters' two subsidiaries in November 1936. Thus in the year preceding the company's first public accounts it moved from owning 1 subsidiary and 3 associates to owning 6 subsidiaries and 3 associates.

Ownership Structure

Just prior to the company's listing application its paid up capital was comprised of:

266,500 fully paid £1 ordinary shares
40,000 fully paid £1 6% cumulative preference shares.

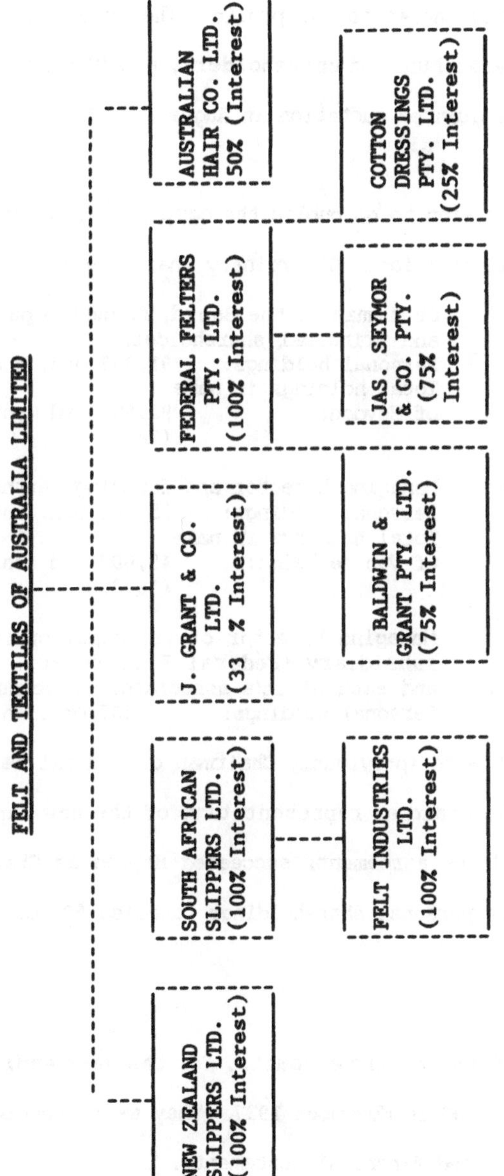
FELT AND TEXTILES OF AUSTRALIA LIMITED
NEW ZEALAND SLIPPERS LTD. (100% Interest)
SOUTH AFRICAN SLIPPERS LTD. (100% Interest)
J. GRANT & CO. LTD. (33 % Interest)
FEDERAL FELTERS PTY. LTD. (100% Interest)
AUSTRALIAN HAIR CO. LTD. 50% (Interest)
FELT INDUSTRIES LTD. (100% Interest)
BALDWIN & GRANT PTY. LTD. (75% Interest)
JAS. SEYMOR & CO. PTY. (75% Interest)
COTTON DRESSINGS PTY. LTD. (25% Interest)

The ordinary shares were held by 36 shareholders. The company's decision to go public was accompanied by the issue of 110,000 fully paid £1 ordinary shares to the public. The issue was fully subscribed, by several hundred shareholders, and the company's ordinary shares were granted quotation in August, 1937.

Management

Prior to the decision to go public the company was managed by three Directors (qualifications 500 ordinary shares) viz:

J.K. Heydon	-	Chairman of the Board, founding partner and principal shareholder. Personal holdings: 91,052 ord. shares. Total holdings in name of Heydon: 92,552 ord. shares (34.73%)
H. Van de Velde	-	Managing Director and founding partner. Personal holdings: 15,002 ord. shares Total holdings in name of Van de Velde: 45,002 ord. shares (16.89%)
A.J. Vale	-	Managing Director of principal operating subsidiary (Federal Felters Pty. Ltd.) and each of it's associated concerns. Personal holdings: 502 ord. shares

Sir W. Massey-Greene (previously Chairman of Federal Felters Pty. Ltd.) joined the board as representative of the new capital being subscribed and, by agreement, succeeded Heydon as Chairman of the company.[1] His personal shareholdings totalled 500 ordinary shares.

Financial Reporting

The company's first public accounts, for the year ending 30 June, 1937, were released in November 1937. They were accompanied by unaudited consolidated financial statements.

---

1. Blainey (1976, p.2) describes Massey-Greene as one of the best known "trustee" directors of the 1930's.

Contracts in force

Debt: Equitable mortgage covering bank overdrafts with the Bank of New South Wales - supported by cross-guarantees. The company's articles contained no borrowing restrictions.

Equity: Articles of Association contain no explicit requirement to consolidate.

Management: Service Agreement between Felt and Textiles of Australia Ltd and H. Van de Velde (February 1937). Paragraphs 5 and 6 of this agreement follow:

5. In addition to the said fixed salary the Managing Director shall during his tenure of office as Managing Director be paid annually from the 1st January 1937 a commission equal to 10 per centum on the following:-

   (1) The annual nett aggregate trading profits from the 1st January 1937 of the Company and all Subsidiary Companies as hereinafter defined.

   (2) The dividends and/or interest received after the 1st January 1937 by the Company and/or its Subsidiary Companies in respect of its or their shareholding in or advances to any Company not being the Company or a subsidiary. Provided that any such dividend shall have been paid out of profits earned subsequent to the 31st day of December 1936 and that any such interest shall be in respect of a period subsequent to the 31st day of December 1936.

   (3) The nominal amount of any distribution of bonus shares received by the Company and all subsidiary companies from trading profits earned subsequent to 1st January 1937.

   "Nett aggregate trading profits" wherever expressed in this Agreement means the nett trading profits after deducting the annual trading loss or losses (if any) of the Company or any one or more of its Subsidiary Companies.

6. For the purposes of this Agreement the nett annual trading profits of the Company and of any Subsidiary Company shall be the nett trading profits of such Companies after deducting:-

   (a) All usual charges and expenses of the business including the fixed remuneration and fees of Directors and salaries of employees including the Fixed salary of the Managing Director and the commission payable to the Managing Director in respect of the profits of the Company of such financial year.

(b) All commission or percentage of profits payable to any employee other than the Managing Director of the Company or any Subsidiary Company subject nevertheless to the provisions of the last preceding sub-paragraph.

(c) All commissions, discounts, interest, bad debts, rates, taxes, outgoings, repairs, depreciation of assets, amortisation, obsolescence and all other like charges and allowances which in the opinion of the Auditors of the Company are usual and necessary in arriving at nett profits.

(d) All income and other taxes or duties including those for the time being charged upon or payable in respect of or measured by or affecting the profits of the Company and its subsidiaries.

PROVIDED ALWAYS that any profits dividends or interest upon which the commission has been calculated shall not again be taken into account for the purpose of computing commission.

Summary

In this case consolidation follows closely substantive changes in:

(i) the firm's operating structure,

(ii) the distribution of the firms ownership (though not control),

(iii) the extension of cross-guarantees, and

(iv) the writing of a compensation plan for the managing director based on "group" performance which requires the elimination of double counting.

Principal References

Felt and Textiles of Australia Ltd:	Prospectus (February 1937) Service Agreement (February 1937)
Sydney Stock Exchange Reference:	A254.
Sydney Stock Exchange Official Gazette:	1937, pp.64, 200, 231.

CASE STUDY NO.7

British Tobacco Company (Australia) Ltd.

Background

Though established and listed in England in 1904 this company has always been run by directors sitting in Australia. Following an adverse decision in the English courts in 1927 regarding the incidence of taxation it was decided that the company should be wound up and the assets transferred to Consolidated Investment Company Ltd, a company incorporated in N.S.W. The old company went into voluntary liquidation in December 1927, whereupon Consolidated Investment changed its name to British Tobacco Company (Australia) Ltd. The company grew modestly and acquired another operating subsidiary in 1940. It was not until the decade of the 1950's that the company resorted frequently to the capital markets for additional funds of any kind.

Operating Structure

The basic operating structure of the company remained unchanged throughout the reconstruction. The parent acted as a pure holding company owning all (but signatory shares) in 3 substantial operating subsidiaries viz:

British Tobacco (Australia) Ltd

W.D. & H.O. Wills (Australia) Ltd (100% interest)	S.T. Leigh & Co. Pty. Ltd (100% interest)	The British Australasian Tobacco Co. Pty. Ltd. (100% interest)

As is the case with the ownership structure (below) this framework remained unchanged until the acquisition of all of the issued shares (excluding preference shares) in Carreras Pty. Ltd. in 1940.

Ownership

Paid up capital of the reconstructed company was:

8,134,459 £1 fully paid ordinary shares
1,484,727 £1 fully paid 6.5% cumulative preference shares.

Some 8,072,192 of the ordinary shares were issued to vendors of the old company as consideration of the assets acquired; as were most of the preference shares. This structure was to remain unchanged until 1940 when additional preference capital was issued for Carreras. At this time 'B' ordinary shares were also issued. While the distribution of this ownership is not ascertainable by 1928 both preferences and ordinaries were listed Australia-wide and in London.

Management

The companies 10 directors (qualifications 1000 shares) remained unchanged through the reorganization in 1927. By the year of the company's first consolidation (1937) the Board had been reduced to 8 members, 4 of whom were members of the original Board.

Financial Reporting

The company's financial statements for the year ending October 1937 were released in November 1937. They contained only the parent company's accounts. However in the Secretary's letter which accompanied these accounts to shareholders it is stated:

> With reference to the Statement made by the Chairman at the last Annual General Meeting, viz., that the Directors would consider the question of supplying shareholders direct with information in regard to our Subsidiary Companies, the Directors have decided to furnish Ordinary Shareholders with a Consolidated Statement of Assets and Liabilities in the form of a balance sheet of British Tobacco Company (Australia) Limited and its Subsidiary Companies. The figures required, however, for this Statement will not be

> available until late in January, 1938.... Copies of the beforementioned Statement will be posted to Ordinary Shareholders as soon as it is completed.

An audited consolidated balance sheet as at October, 1937 was released in February 1938.

Contracts in Force

Debt: The company was very lightly geared and there is no evidence of any contingent liabilities under guarantees.

Management: No evidence available.

Equity: Despite considerable concern being expressed by the Secretaries of both the Melbourne (Correspondence, 13.12.27) and Sydney (Correspondence, 23.5.28) Stock Exchanges the company was ultimately listed under its old (pre-1927) articles. The following extracts from the Sydney Secretary's letter are illustrative:

> My Chairman and some of the company's directors have had several conferences regarding listing, but difficulty in reaching finality has been encountered by reason of the Stock Exchange requirement which provides that holding companies shall issue balance sheets and profit and loss accounts of their subsidiaries. The directors of the British Tobacco Co. (which is purely a holding company) are not disposed to comply with such requirement, and point out that the London Stock Exchange has granted quotation to both their ordinary and preference shares in the New Co. without requiring any more information in the accounts than previously supplied, i.e., without requiring the disclosure of any information regarding the assets and liabilities or profits and losses of the subsidiaries.
>
> However, with particular reference to the British Tobacco Co. - My Committee have given much consideration to the question of listing, and are of opinion that the best interests would be served by regarding the company not as a new enterprise but as a continuance of the old undertaking. On that foundation they suggest that we follow the London Stock Exchange and list the company without insisting upon alterations to its Articles of Association, which are in effect a repetition of the previously existing regulations.

Summary

In this case consolidation follows closely substantive changes in the firm's management. The death of the Chairman and the retirement of another of the original directors resulted in the Board dropping from ten to eight. Only 4 of these eight were members of the Board at the time of the concerns expressed in the correspondence referred to above (i.e., only 4 can be clearly identified as opposing consolidation). At the same time it appears as though the Directors were under pressure from shareholders for additional disclosures (e.g., comments at preceding two annual general meetings).

Principal References

British Tobacco Company (Australia) Ltd :
Correspondence, Melbourne Stock Exchange : 13 December, 1927
Correspondence, Sydney Stock Exchange : 23 May, 1928

Sydney Stock Exchange Reference : A239

Melbourne Stock Exchange Official Record : January, 1937, p.21.

CASE STUDY NO.8

Schute Bell Badgery Lumby Ltd.

Background

This company was formed in 1937 to takeover and amalgamate the businesses of Schute, Bell and Company Ltd. (wool and produce brokers) and Keith Badgery and Lumby Ltd. (stock and property salesmen) by the purchase of the whole of the issue share capital of the former and the whole of the assets of the latter. The company traded profitably until taken over by N.Z.L. Holdings (Aust.) Pty. Ltd. in 1948.

Operating Structure

The company's first balance sheet reveals that in the process of amalgamation it was considered desirable to leave the old company of Schute Bell and Co. Ltd. in existence since:

> ...by doing this, and such company retaining its fixed assets, considerable savings were effected in Stamp Duty and Government fees etc.

Ownership Structure

The company was listed in July 1937 with an issued and paid up capital comprised of:

30,750 £1 ordinary shares credited as fully paid to holders of shares in Schute Bell and Co. Ltd.
10,100 £1 ordinary shares credited as fully paid to holders of Shares in Badgery and Lumby Ltd.
44,150 £1 ordinary shares issued to the public
85,000 shares

The issue of shares to the public was fully subscribed and the number of shareholders in the new organization was 179. Apart from the holdings of the Directors (see below) there was only one other substantial shareholding (Schute, 3375 or 4%).

Management

The company was set up with five "managing" directors, each employed as an operating manager of a division of the combined operations, viz:

F.R. Moser	5060 ord. shares (6%)
J.W. Walker	2997 ord. shares (3.5%)
R. Ruwald	2718 ord. shares (3.2%)
K. Badgery	7783 ord. shares (9.2%)
W.G. Lumby	1201 ord. shares (1.4%)

The first three named Directors had held "managing" directorships in the same functional areas in Schute Bell; the latter two directors the same positions in Badgery and Lumby. Directors qualifications were 500 ordinary shares.

Financial Reporting

The combined company released its first public accounts for the year ending June 1937 in August, 1937. It submitted both an audited consolidated balance sheet and profit and loss account supported by the individual audited accounts of each company. However, in the next financial year and thereafter, the company reverted (without explanation) to the presentation of separate parent and subsidiary accounts.

Contracts in force

Debt: The Company's articles contained no borrowing restriction. There were no significant creditors in 1937.

Management: The articles provided that the Managing Director (only) may be remunerated by way of salary, commission or participation in profits (or any or all of these modes). However there was no evidence relating to any Managing Directors service agreement (the implication, in fact, seems to be the opposite).

<u>Equity</u>: The company's articles had been modified prior to listing to comply with the list requirements. The latter did not require consolidated statements (refer Chapter 2.1.2)

Summary

In this instance consolidation follows closely substantive changes in:

(i) the firm's operating structure, and

(ii) the distribution of the firm's ownership (though not control).

Principal References

Schute Bell Badgery Lumby Ltd : Prospectus (7 April, 1937)

Sydney Stock Exchange Reference: 317

CASE STUDY NO.9

Repco Ltd.

Background

The company was incorporated in September 1937 in Victoria as a holding company to takeover the capital of two operating subsidiaries. Its principal function was to raise funds for these subsidiaries which had been operating successfully from as early as 1921 (Auto Grinding Co. Pty. Ltd.) and 1926 (Replacement Parts Pty. Ltd.). The introduction of further capital on the formation of the holding company resulted in a period of rapid expansion.

Operating Structure

The figure indicates the group structure at the time of formation of the public company:

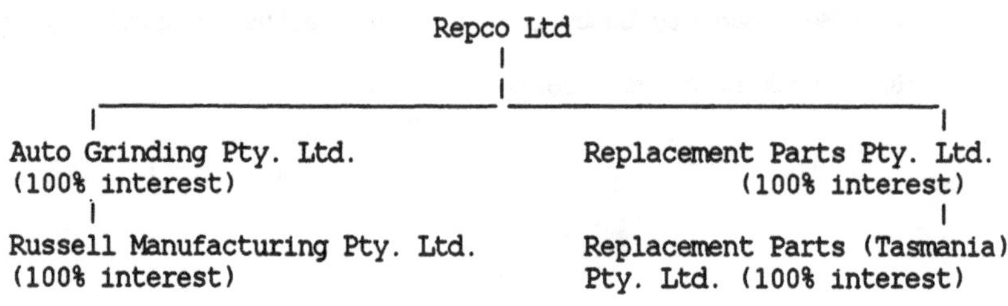

Ownership

All of the private companies concerned had been founded, owned and managed by Mr. R.G. Russell. The public company was formed with an issued capital of 300,000 £1 fully paid ordinary shares, of which Russell received 200,000 shares as consideration for the private companies and 100,000 shares were offered to the public. The ordinary shares were listed in Melbourne late in 1937.

Management

The board of Directors of the public company was comprised as follows:

R.G. Russell	-	Managing Director, founder and principal shareholder Personal holdings:	200,000 ord. shares (66.7%)
O.R. Wadds	-	Director and manager of Replacement Parts Pty Ltd. Personal holdings:	500 ord. shares (0.17%)
W.R. Richardson	-	Director and external engineering consultant to the group. Personal holdings:	500 ord. shares (0.17%)
J.E. Martin	-	Director, underwriter for and representative of, ordinary (public) shareholders. Personal holdings:	500 ord. shares (0.17%)

Financial Reporting

The company's first public accounts for the financial year ending September 1938 were released in October 1938. They were accompanied by a set of consolidated financial statements. The consolidated balance sheet was audited.

Contracts in Force

Debt: Overdrafts with National Bank of Australasia Ltd existed in the subsidiary companies (no contingent liabilities disclosed).

Management: Managing Director under agreement to serve for 10 years - no other details.

Equity: Articles of Association not available.

Summary

In this case consolidation follows closely substantive changes in the distribution of ownership of the company (though not in its control).

Principal References

Repco Ltd:	Prospectus (September 1937)
Sydney Stock Exchange Reference:	R15A.

CASE STUDY NO.10

Consolidated Fibre Products

Background

Registered in Victoria in August 1938 to takeover the operations of a company of the same name which had been incorporated in 1935 to acquire all of the issued capital in Egg Fillers and Containers (Aust) Pty. Ltd., the Carton Co. Pty. Ltd. and Vicker Engineering Pty. Ltd. The vendor company had operated successfully since incorporation and continued expansion brought the company to the market in July 1938.

Operating Structure

The new company held all of the issued share capital in 3 operating subsidiaries. In addition it carried on the business of pulp moulder and distributor of its subsidiaries products.

Ownership Structure

The purchase price of the old company was satisfied by the issue of 55,000 £1 fully paid ordinary shares in the new company. In addition 25,000 £1 7.5% cumulative preference shares were issued to the public. The preference shares were granted quotation late in 1938. The ordinary shares were held largely by the founder and managing director of the vendor company; who took on the same role in the new company.

Management

The new company was managed by three directors (qualifications 300 shares) viz:

S. Meltzer	-	Managing Director, founder and principal shareholder Personal holdings:	47,000 ord. shares (85.5%)
W.G. Norman	-	Chairman of Directors and founding director of predecessor company. Personal holdings:	1998 ord. shares (3.6%)
D.A. Prentice	-	Director, underwriter for and representative of, the preference shareholders.	

Financial Reporting

The company's first public accounts, for the year ending December 1938 were released in March 1939 and were accompanied by a set of consolidated financial statements. The consolidated balance sheet was audited.

Contracts in Force

Debt: The company had relied heavily on shareholder loans and the first accounts reveal no "external" debt other than trade creditors.
No borrowing restrictions in Articles of Association.

Management: No evidence available but paragraph 128(g) of the Articles of Association specified:

> The remuneration of the Managing Director shall from time to time be fixed by the Directors and may be by way of fixed salary or commission on dividends or profits of the company or of any other company in which the company is directly or through a subsidiary company interested or by participation in any such profits or by any or all of those modes or the remuneration may be divided between the Company and its subsidiary companies or any of them as the Directors may determine.

Equity: Paragraph 51 of the Articles of Association requires:

> The Directors shall also lay before the Company at the Annual Ordinary General Meeting in each year a consolidated profit and loss account and Balance-sheet of such subsidiary Companies in which it has a controlling interest.

Summary

The company's decision to raise public funds through a preference share issue was followed by the release of consolidated accounts - as required by the articles of the recently incorporated organisation (but not the Stock Exchange Listing Requirements of the time).

Principal References

Consolidated Fibre Products Ltd: Prospectus (July 1938).

Sydney Stock Exchange Reference : C23

CASE STUDY NO.11

Bradford Cotton Mills Ltd.

Background

The company was registered in N.S.W. in 1927 with a capital of 75,906 £1 fully paid ordinary shares and a purely local sphere of operations concentrated on the weaving industry. By 1932 modest growth had resulted in the establishment of its own spinning mill and dye house. In 1935 the company started to expand rapidly and it approached the market for funds (preference shares) for the first time. The company went to the market for funds (ordinary shares) again in 1937 and 1938. In anticipation of yet further expansion the company established two subsidiaries, C & D Mills Pty. Ltd. and Sanforizing Services of Australia Pty. Ltd. in early 1939. Finance for these developments was provided largely by the issue of second cumulative preference shares. In July 1937 Bradford announced merger negotiations were taking place with Austral Silk and Cotton Mills Ltd. The merger was consummated in October 1939 with the issue of both ordinary and preference shares in Bradford for all but 180 of the ordinary shares in Austral. By 1940 Bradford was one of the largest manufacturers of cotton textiles in Australia. It had substantial operations in both N.S.W. and Victoria and faced the prospect of continued rapid growth. Jobson's Investment Digest identified the company as having "outstanding prospects".

Operating Structure

As indicated above the company's rapid expansion resulted in the establishment of its first two wholly-owned subsidiaries in 1939, immediately preceding the release of its first consolidated accounts. Shortly after the close of the 1939 financial year the company acquired another, much larger, subsidiary - Austral Silk and Cotton Mills.

Ownership Structure

At the time of the listing of the company's preference shares in April 1935 the paid up capital of the company comprised:

75,906 £1 fully paid ordinary shares
40,000 £1 fully paid 6% first cumulative preference shares.

The ordinary shares were held by 13 shareholders, the preference shares by 41 shareholders. By February 1937 the number of ordinary shares had increased to 107,500. These shares were listed at this time and held by 43 shareholders. By October 1939, following the issue of shares for Austral Silk and Cotton Mills, Bradford had several hundred shareholders.

Management

Details of the company's management and their respective shareholdings at various points in time appear below (Directors qualifications 250 ordinary shares):

	April 1935		February 1937	
	Ord.Shs. (%)	Pref.Shs (%)	Ord.Shs. (%)	Pref.Shs. (%)
F.M. Keighley	35,715 (47%)	7,650 (19%)	34,713 (32%)	7,650 (19%)
A.W. Keighley	35,715 (47%)	2,650 (6.6%)	43,496 (40%)	2,650 (6.6%)
Name of Keighley	-	11,500 (28.8%)	3,500 (3.3%)	11,500 (28.8%)
R.H. Treacy	1,680 (2%)	400 (1%)	2,319 (2%)	400 (1%)
R.J. Webster	-	-	12,500 (11.6%)	-
Totals shares	75,906 (100%)	40,000 (100%)	107,500 (100%)	40,000 (100%)

F.M. Keighley was founder and managing director until April 1937 when his brother, A.W. Keighley, assumed this position. F.M. Keighley remained on as a director and R.J. Webster joined the Board as Chairman of Directors. By the time the company had released its 1939 accounts A. Van De Velde (Managing Director, Felt and Textiles of Australia Ltd.) had also been appointed to the Board.[1] Subsequent to the release of these accounts and as a consequence of the Austral takeover Sir W. Massey-Greene (Director, Austral Silk and Cotton Mills Ltd., Felt and Textiles of Australia Ltd.) was appointed Chairman of the Bradford Board. Treacy resigned to go to the Board of Sydney Cotton Mills in October 1938.

Financial Reporting

The company's accounts for financial 1939, released in September 1939, were accompanied by a set of consolidated financial statements. The consolidated balance sheet was audited.

Contracts in force

Debt: Guarantees in respects of Bank overdrafts of subsidiaries. The company's articles contained no borrowing restrictions.

Management: While the company's articles (para. 104) specifically provided that the Managing Director could be remunerated by way of salary, commission or participation in profits (or any or all of these modes), no evidence was available relating to the Managing Director's service agreement.

Equity: The articles of association (paras 140-145) specified that the Directors were to provide to shareholders and to place before the general meeting a profit and loss account and a balance-sheet accompanied by a report of the Directors. Paragraph 146 required:

---

1. Refer Case Study No.6. Van de Velde's own company had consolidated in 1937.

> Together with every such balance-sheet the Company shall furnish shareholders (other than holders of Employees' shares) with a printed balance-sheet and profit and loss account of any subsidiary company in which the Company has a controlling interest but in the event of the Company having a controlling interest in more than one subsidiary company the Company may furnish the shareholders with an aggregate printed balance-sheet and profit and loss account of the Company and of the subsidiary companies.

Summary

In this case consolidation follows closely substantial changes in:

(i) the firm's operating structure,

(ii) the distribution of the firm's ownership (though not control),

(iii) the effecting of a set of cross-guarantees, and

(iv) the appointment to the Board of a Director from a company which was already consolidating.

Recall also that the articles adopted by the company (February 1935) immediately prior to listing provided that the company may submit an "aggregate" balance-sheet and profit and loss account.

Principal References:

Bradford Cotton Mill Ltd:	Prospectus (January 1940) Articles of Association (February 1940)
Sydney Stock Exchange Reference:	E87
Jobson's Investment Digest:	December 16, 1940.

APPENDIX III

Corporate Income Taxation in Australia 1930 - 1962

Up to and including the income year ended 30 June 1941 Australian companies were subject to both Commonwealth and State income taxes on their taxable incomes. State income taxes were suspended thereafter and the Commonwealth became (and remained) the sole income taxing authority.[1] Tables 1 and 2 summarize, respectively, the tax regimes in force in the pre and post - June 1941 periods. Since the first Australian consolidation occurred in 1931 the starting point for subsequent discussion was set as the financial (and income) year 1929/30. Further, since the thesis is concerned with the reporting practices of (listed) public companies only the tax rates applicable thereto appear in the Tables. Reference to private company rates will be made as and when appropriate.

When the Committee on Uniform Taxation submitted its report in March, 1942 there were 26 separate income taxes in Australia. It was technically possible for a taxpayer's marginal and average rate of taxation to exceed 20 shillings in the pound (i.e., 100 percent)[2]. Table 1 indicates the multiplicity of taxes levied upon the income of public companies in NSW and Victoria over the decade of the 1930's.

---

1. The circumstances surrounding this radical change in the tax structure are detailed in Laffer (1942), Carlaw (1942), Bailey (1944) and Crivelli (1946). Parsons, (1967) contains an overview of the Commonwealth's taxation system from its inception in 1915.

2. Refer Laffer (1942, pp.170-173). Hereafter all references to pounds, shilling and pence have been converted to equivalent dollar rates.

APPENDIX III - TABLE 1

Primary Rates of Income Tax Payable by Public Companies in NSW and Victoria 1929-30 to 1940-41

Year of Income	Taxing Authority		
	Victoria (%)	New South Wales (%)	Commonwealth (%)
1929-30	8.75[1]	Sliding Scale [2]	6.67[4]
1930-31	8.75[1]	Sliding Scale [2]	7.08[4]
1931-32	8.75[1]	Sliding Scale [2]	7.08[4]
1932-33	8.75[1]	Sliding Scale [1]	5.0 [4]
1933-34	8.75[1]	Sliding Scale [1]	5.0 [4]
1934-35	8.75[1]	Sliding Scale [1]	5.0 [4]
1935-36	8.75[1]	11.25 [1]	5.0
1936-37	8.75[1]	11.25 [1]	5.0
1937-38	9.58	11.25 [1]	5.8
1938-39	9.58	12.5	10.0
1939-40	10.0	12.5	10.0 [3]
1940-41	10.0	15.0 [3]	20.0 [3,5,6]

Sources: (Commonwealth) Income Tax Act, 1929 to 1940
(NSW) Income Tax Act, 1928, 1936, 1939, 1941
(NSW) Unemployment Relief (Tax) Act, 1930, 1931, 1932
(NSW) Special Income and Wages Tax Act, 1933 to 1938
(Victoria) Income Tax Act, 1928, 1931 to 1935
(Victoria) Income Tax (Rates) Act, 1936 to 1940

Notes to Table:

1. Special Income Tax also levied
2. Unemployment Relief Tax also levied
3. Undistributed Profits Tax also levied
4. Special Property Income Tax also levied
5. Super-tax also levied
6. War-time (Company) tax also levied

For most of the decade of the 1930's the State of Victoria assessed companies to income tax at the flat rate of 9.58 cents in the $. While the primary rate was 8.75 percent, an additional tax of 7.5 percent of the total tax payable at the primary rate, increased the overall rate to 9.58 percent. In the two years immediately preceding uniform taxation the overall rate rose to 10 percent.

N.S.W levied corporate income tax on a sliding scale between 1927/28 and 1934/35. The rates were initially set at 10 percent on an income of less than $1,000 and increased by regular gradations to 13.3 percent on incomes of less than $9,000, at which level the rate remained constant. In 1932/33 the rates were lowered by 1.25 percent all round. As in Victoria, a number of other special taxes existed. Between 1929/30 and 1931/32 an Unemployment Relief Tax - set in its first year at 1.25 percent and in each of the remaining years at 5.0 percent - was levied on corporate income. In 1932/33 this tax was replaced by a Special Income Tax levied at the rate of 5.0 percent on the first 5/12 of net assessable income, 4.2 percent on the remainder. In 1933/34 this rate was changed to 4.2 percent on net assessable income, and it remained at this level until the tax was removed in 1938/39. Between 1935/36 and 1940/41 income tax was levied at the flat rates indicated in Table 1. Just prior to the introduction of uniform taxation this rate reached 15 percent. Additionally, there was an undistributed profits tax of 5 percent for public companies (retention allowance 50 per cent).[3]

The Commonwealth first levied an income tax in 1915. Between 1930-1940 it did so at the flat rates indicated in Table 1. Over the first half of this decade the Commonwealth also levied a special tax on income from property (including inter-company dividends) at rates which, over time, ranged from 5.0 to 10.0 percent. For the income year ended June 1940 the Commonwealth reintroduced an undistributed profits tax at the flat rate of 10 percent on non-private companies with a retention allowance of 25 percent.[4] This tax remained in place until 1951-52. With the onset of World War II the Commonwealth introduced two new taxes. The first was a super-tax, set at 5.0 percent on taxable income in excess of $10,000. The second was a special war-time company tax, which was levied at an increasing rate (rising initially to 60 subsequently to 78 percent) on the amount by which taxable income exceeded a "percentage standard" (set initially at 8 and subsequently reduced to 5 percent). This standard was related to "capital employed" and rules for the determination of the latter were prescribed. These taxes remained in force until 1951/52 and 1945/46 respectively (see also Table 2). However, during the war years companies were required to pay only the higher of the two.

---

3. An undistributed profits tax had existed for many years for "private companies". In fact, as was the case in Victoria, over this decade the distinction between public and private companies was only relevant for the purpose of calculating the undistributed profits tax. Both types of company faced the same primary rates of taxation indicated in Table 1.

4. The Commonwealth Commissioner had possessed the power to assess all companies to undistributed profits tax between 1915 and 1933, but as a matter of practicality had only ever done so on private companies. This practice was formalised in the 1934 Act which set up the private/public dichotomy.

APPENDIX III - TABLE 2

Primary Rates of Income tax Payable by Australian Public Companies 1941-42 to 1961-62

Year of Income	Taxing Authority Commonwealth (%)	
1941-42 to 1946-47	30%	1,2,3
1947-48 to 1949-50	25% on first $10,000 30% thereafter	1,3
1950-51	35%	1,3
1951-52	25% on first $1,000 35% thereafter	1,3
1952-53 to 1954-55	30% on first $10,000 35% thereafter	
1955 - 56	35% on first $10,000 40% thereafter	
1956-57 to 1958-59	32.5% on first $10,000 37.5% thereafter	
1959-60 to 1961-62	35% on first $10,000 40% thereafter	

Source: Income Tax Act, 1941 to 1955
Income Tax and Social Services Contribution (Companies) Act, 1956
Income Tax and Social Services Contribution Act, 1957 to 1962

Notes to Table:

1. Super-tax at 5.0 percent on all taxable income excess of $10,000, rises to 10.0 percent from 1950-51.
2. War-time company tax based on "percentage standard" - assessed until 1945-46.
3. Undistributed profits tax of 10.0 percent also levied.

Table 2 summarizes the primary rates of tax payable by public companies since the introduction of uniform taxation. The primary rates are self-explanatory and the super and war-time taxes have already been discussed. Only two essential features of the system remain to be considered. The first, which is apparent in Table 2, is the step in the tax scale which was introduced in 1947-48 and, with one exception (1950-51), remained in force until 1970-71. The second, which is not apparent from the Table, is the differential tax rate between public and private companies which was introduced into the Commonwealth legislation in 1950-51 and, with one exception (1951-52), remained in force until 1974-75.[5]

---

5. Between 1950-51 and 1960-62 private company taxation rates were 10.0 percent lower on the first $10,000, 5.0 percent lower thereafter.

REFERENCES

Aitken, M.J. and D.J. Stokes, "Influences on the Demand for External Audits by Australian Companies," unpublished manuscript, University of New South Wales (August 1984).

Armitage, J.K., "The Debenture Trust Deed," in Committee for Post-Graduate Studies in the Department of Law, Public Company Finance (University of Sydney, November 1981).

Bailey, K.H., "The Uniform Income Tax Plan," The Economic Record (December 1944), pp.170-188.

Barnea, A., R.A. Haugen and L.W. Senbet, "Market Imperfections, Agency Problems and Capital Structure: A Review," Financial Management (Summer 1981), pp.7-22.

Beaver, W.H., Financial Reporting: An Accounting Revolution, (Prentice-Hall, Inc., Englewood Cliffs, N.J., 1981).

Blainey, G., The Politics of Big Business: A History, The Academy of Social Sciences in Australia Annual Lecture, Canberra, (November 1976).

Bowen, R.M., Noreen E.W. and J.M. Lacey, "Determinants of the Corporate Decision to Capitalize Interest," Journal of Accounting and Economics (August 1981), pp.151-179.

Campbell, D.T. and J.C. Stanley, Experimental and Quasi-Experimental Designs for Research (Rand McNally, Chicago, 1966).

Carlaw, H.S., "The Uniform Income Tax in Australia," The Economic Record (December 1942), pp.158-167.

Chambers, R.J., "Capital for Private Enterprise under Existing Economic Conditions" paper presented at the Australian Society of Accountants Convention on Accounting, Adelaide, (31 May - 4 June, 1954).

Chow, C.W., "The Demand for External Auditing: Size, Debt and Ownership Influences," The Accounting Review (April 1982), pp.272-291.

Collins, C.M., Australian Company Law (The Law Book Company of Australasia Pty. Ltd., Sydney, 1940).

Crivelli, R.L., "The Euthanasia of the States," The Australian Quarterly (June 1946), pp.35-42.

Desiatnik, R.J., Guidebook to Australian State Payroll Tax, (C.C.H. Australia Ltd, Sydney, 1973).

Edwards, J.R. and K.M. Webb, "The Development of Group Accounting in the United Kingdom to 1933," The Accounting Historians Journal (Spring 1984), pp.31-61.

Editorial, "Holding and Subsidiary Companies," The Commonwealth Journal of Accountancy (December 1933), pp.85-87.

Evans, E.J., Prospectuses and Annual Reports: An Historical Look at Rule Development, New England Accounting Research Study No.3., University of New England, Armidale, 1974.

Ewart, G.M., "The Published Accounts of Holding Companies," The Chartered Accountant in Australia (January 1948), pp.463-488.

Fama, E.F., "Agency Problems and the Theory of the Firm," Journal of Political Economy (April 1980), pp.228-307.

Farquharson, D., Guarantees (University of Queensland Press, Brisbane, 1956).

Ferguson, D.M., "The Published Accounts of Holding Companies," The Accountant in Australia (March-April, 1931), pp.152-154, 200-207.

Finn, M.A. and E.G. Payne, Taxation of Company Groups (Taxation Institute of Australia, Sydney, 1977).

Fitzgerald, A.A., "Australian Company Legislation," (Editorial), The Australian Accountant (September 1936), p.99.

Fitzgerald, A.A., "Published Accounts of Companies under the Victorian Companies Act, 1938," The Australian Accountant (March 1939), pp.85-92.

Fitzgerald, A.A., "Recommendations on Accounting Principles," The Australian Accountant (June 1944), pp.179-182.

Fitzgerald, A.A., "Trends in Company Financing," in Investment in Australia Symposium, Melbourne Stock Exchange, Melbourne, (February 1965).

Fitzgerald, G.E., "The Accounts of Holding Companies," The Australian Accountant (March 1938), pp.137-159.

Fitzgerald, G.E., "Holding Companies," The Australian Accountant (November 1950 - January 1951), passim.

Fitzgerald, G.E. and A.E. Speck, "The Accounts of Holding Companies," The Australian Accountant (December, 1944 - May 1945), passim.

Foster, G., "Accounting Policy Decisions and Capital Market Research," Journal of Accounting and Economics (March 1980), pp.29-62.

Gibson, R.W., Standards of Disclosure in Published Reports of Australian Public Companies, Masters Thesis, University of Melbourne, Melbourne, (September 1967).

Gibson, R.W., Disclosure by Australian Companies (Melbourne University Press, Melbourne, 1971).

Goldberg, L., The Florescent Decade: Accounting Education in Australia 1945-1955 (Accounting Association of Australia and New Zealand, Melbourne, 1981).

Goldberg, L. and D.M. Hocking, "Holding Companies in Australia," paper presented at ANZAAS Conference, Hobart, (January 1949).

Gole, V.L., Australian Proprietary Companies: Management, Finance and Taxation (Butterworth and Co., Sydney, 1970).

Gower, L.C.B., The Principles of Modern Company Law (Stevens and Sons, London, 1969).

Graham, A.W., Without Fear or Favour: A History of The Institute of Chartered Accountants in Australia 1928-1978 (Butterworths Pty. Ltd., Sydney, 1978).

Grimwood, E.L., "Unsecured Notes and Deposits as a Source of Company Finance," Australian Accountancy Student (March 1960), pp.7-12.

Gunn, J.A.L., Gunn's Commonwealth Income Tax: Law and Practice (Butterworth and Company, Sydney, 1948).

Gunn, J.A.L. and M. Mass, Payroll Tax in Australia (Butterworth and Co., Sydney, 1961).

Hall, A.R., Australian Company Finance: Sources and Uses of Funds of Public Companies, 1946-1955, A.N.U. Social Science Monograph 7 (Canberra 1956).

Hagerman, R.L. and M.E. Zmijewski, "Some Economic Determinants of Accounting Policy Choice," Journal of Accounting and Economics (August 1979), pp.141-161.

Henderson, R.F., "Notes on the Australian Capital Market, 1946-53," The Economic Record (November 1954), pp.172-186.

Hirst, R.R., "The Development Institutions," in R.R. Hirst and R.H. Wallace (eds.) Studies in the Australian Capital Market (F.W. Cheshire Pty. Ltd. 1964), pp.303-345.

Holthausen, R.W. and R.W. Leftwich, "The Economic Consequences of Accounting Choice: Implications of Costly Contracting and Monitoring," Journal of Accounting and Economics (August 1983), pp.77-117.

Ijiri, Y., Theory of Accounting Measurement, Studies in Accounting Research No.10 (American Accounting Association, 1975).

Irish, R.A., "Holding Companies and their Subsidiaries," The Australian Accountant (September 1943), pp.342-353.

Jensen, M.C. and W.H. Meckling, "Theory of the Firm: Managerial Behavior, Agency Costs and Ownership Structure," Journal of Financial Economics (October 1976), pp.305-360.

Keown, K.C., "The Capital Structure of Australian Companies," The Australian Accountant (September 1952), pp.287-303.

Keown, K.C., "The Finance of Company Expansion," Australian Accountancy Student (September 1954), pp.71-81.

Kitchen, J., "The Accounts of British Holding Company Groups: Some thoughts on development in the early years," Accounting and Business Research (Spring 1972), pp.114-136.

Kitchen, J. and R.H. Parker, Accounting Thought and Education: Six English Pioneers (The Institute of Chartered Accountants in England and Wales, London, 1980).

Laffer, K.M., "Taxation Reform in Australia," The Economic Record (December 1942), pp.168-179.

Leftwich, R., "Accounting Information in Private Markets: Evidence from Private Lending Agreements," The Accounting Review (January 1983), pp.23-42.

Leftwich, R.W., Watts, R.L. and J.L. Zimmerman, "Voluntary Corporate Disclosure: The Case of Interim Reporting," Journal of Accounting Research (Supplement 1981), pp.50-77.

Ma, R. and R.H. Parker, Consolidation Accounting in Australia (Longman Cheshire Pty. Ltd., Melbourne, 1983).

Mathews, R.L., "Capital for Private Enterprise under Existing Economic Conditions," paper presented at the Australian Society of Accountants' Convention on Accounting (31 May - 4 June 1954).

Mathews, R.L., "The Stock Exchange, Securities and New Issue Markets, Investment Companies and Unit Trusts," in R.R. Hirst and R.H. Wallace (eds.), Studies in the Australian Capital Market, (F.W. Cheshire Pty. Ltd., Melbourne, 1964), pp.1-50.

Mathews, R.L. and G.C. Harcourt, "Company Finance," in R.R. Hirst and R.H. Wallace (eds.), Studies in the Australian Capital Market, (F.W. Cheshire Pty. Ltd., Melbourne, 1964), pp.377-424.

McGee, F.V., "Australian Business Finance," The Economic Record (November 1927), pp.252-265.

McGregor, W.J., "A Report on Progress in the Development of Australian Accounting Standards," The Australian Accountant (November 1984), pp.867-868.

McInnes, R.A., "Capital for Private Enterprise under Existing Economic Conditions," paper presented at the Australian Society of Accountants' Convention on Accounting (31 May - 4 June 1954).

Merton, R.C., "Theory of Rational Option Pricing," Bell Journal of Economics and Management Science (Spring 1973), pp.141-183.

Mumford, D., "The Origins of Consolidated Accounts," University of Lancaster Accounting and Finance Working Paper Series (September 1982).

Myers, S.C., "Determinants of Corporate Borrowing," Journal of Financial Economics (November 1977), pp.147-175.

Nash, G., "Duties of Directors," The Australian Accountant (August 1984), pp.571-573.

Nixon, E.V., "Holding Companies," The Commonwealth Journal of Accountancy (August 1 1928), pp.362-367.

Nobes, C.W. and R.H. Parker, "Chronology of the Development of Company Financial Reporting in Great Britain, 1844-1977," in T.A. Lee, and R.H. Parker (eds.), The Evolution of Corporate Financial Reporting (Thomas Nelson and Sons Ltd., England, 1979), pp.197-207.

O'Dowd, B. and D.I. Menzies, Victorian Company Law and Practice, (The Law Book Company of Australasia Pty. Ltd., Sydney, 1940).

Parsons, R.W., "An Australian View of Corporation Tax," British Tax Review (January/February 1967), pp.14-40.

Porter, K.R., The Mortgage Debenture (The Law Book Company, Sydney, 1970).

Posner, R.A., Economic Analysis of Law (Little, Brown and Company, U.S.A., 1977).

Ross, S.A., "The Determination of Financial Structure: The Incentive - Signalling Approach," The Bell Journal of Economics (Spring 177), pp.23-40.

Ross, S.A., "Disclosure Regulation in Financial Markets: Implications of Modern Finance Theory and Signalling Theory," in F.R. Edwards, (ed.), Issues in Financial Regulation (McGraw-Hill Inc., N.Y., 1979).

Smith, C.W. and J.B. Warner, "On Financial Contracting: An Analysis of Bond Covenants," Journal of Financial Economics (June 1979), pp.117-161.

Smith, C.W. and R.L. Watts, "Incentive and Tax Effects of Executive Compensation Plans," Australian Journal of Management (December 1982), pp.139-157.

Spence, J.D., "Some Aspects of Holding Companies," Australian Accountancy Student (September 1949), pp.183-188.

Spence, J.D., "Consolidated Statements," in G.E. Fitzgerald and K.C. Keown (eds.), Australian Accountancy Progress, 1958 (Butterworth and Company, Sydney, 1958).

Spender, P.C. and G. Wallace, Company Law and Practice (The Law Book Company of Australasia Pty. Ltd., Sydney, 1937).

Verrechia, R.E., "On the Theory of Market Information Efficiency," Journal of Accounting and Economics (March 1979), pp.77-90.

Walker, R.G., Consolidated Statements (Arno Press, N.Y., 1978).

Watts, R.L., "Corporate Financial Statements: A Product of the Market and Political Processes," Australian Journal of Management (April 1977), pp.53-75.

Watts, R.L. and J.L. Zimmerman, "Towards a Positive Theory of the Determination of Accounting Standards," The Accounting Review (January 1978), pp.112-134.

Wheelwright, E.L., Ownership and Control of Australian Companies: a Study of 102 of the Largest Public Companies Incorporated in Australia (The Law Book Company of Australasia Pty. Ltd., Sydney, 1957).

Wheelwright, E.L., Anatomy of Australian Manufacturing Industry: the Ownership and Control of 300 of the Largest Manufacturing Companies in Australia (The Law Book Company, Sydney, 1967).

Whittred, G., "Financial Contracting: Its Dependence on Accounting Information and Its Effect on Management's Choice of Reporting Mechanism," unpublished manuscript, University of New South Wales, Sydney, (October 1983).

Whittred, G. and I. Zimmer, "Accounting Information in the Market for Debt," unpublished manuscript, University of New South Wales, Sydney, (February 1985).

Wilkinson, H.L., The Trust Movement in Australia (Critchley Parker Pty. Ltd., Australia, 1914).

Yorston, R.K., "Consolidated Statements," The Chartered Accountant in Australia (March - September 1947), passim.

Yorston, R.K., Limited Liability Companies in Australia (The Law Book Company of Australasia Pty. Ltd., Sydney, 1956).

Yorston, R.K. and E.E. Fortescue, Australian Secretarial Practice (The Law Book Company of Australasia Pty. Ltd., Sydney, 1953).

Zimmer, I.R., "Accounting for Interest by Real Estate Developers," Journal of Accounting and Economics (January 1986), forthcoming.

Reports of Committees and Commissions (Chronological Order)

Royal Commission on Taxation - Reports (Chairman: W. Warren Kerr); Government Printer, Melbourne, 1921-23.

Royal Commission on Taxation - Reports, (Chairman: D.G. Ferguson), Commonwealth Government Printer, Canberra, 1932-34.

Commonwealth Committee on Taxation - Reports, (Chairman: E.S. Spooner), Commonwealth Government Printer, Canberra, 1951-53.

Committee on Rates of Depreciation - Report, (Chairman: A.S. Hulme), Commonwealth Government Printer, Canberra, 1955.

Commonwealth Committee on Taxation - Report, (Chairman: Sir George Ligertwood), Commonwealth Government Printer, Canberra, 1961.

Taxation Review Committee - Full Report, (Chairman: K.W. Asprey), Australian Government Publishing Service, Canberra, 1975.